Re-Enchanting Christianity

Dave Tomlinson was an influential leader in the house church movement until he found he could no longer accept its approach to theology and spirituality. With his wife, Pat, he founded Holy Joes, an influential meeting place in a pub for all who found regular church boring or unfulfilling.

Now vicar of a thriving and diverse parish in North London, and a regular favourite at the Greenbelt Christian Arts Festival, Dave is the author of the seminal *The Post-Evangelical*. He has an MA in Biblical Interpretation.

Re-Enchanting Christianity

Faith in an emerging culture

Dave Tomlinson

CANTERBURY
PRESS

Norwich

First published in 2008 by the Canterbury Press Norwich
(a publishing imprint of Hymns Ancient & Modern Limited,
a registered charity)
13–17 Long Lane, London EC1A 9PN

www.scm-canterburypress.co.uk

British Library Cataloguing in Publication data

A catalogue record for this book is available
from the British Library

ISBN 978-1-85311-857-9

Typeset by Regent Typesetting, London
Printed and bound in the UK by
CPI Antony Rowe, Chippenham, Wiltshire

Contents

v

For Patty, my lifelong friend and partner,
who resurrected this book when I thought it was dead

Preface

Every day people are straying away from the church and going back to God.

Lenny Bruce

People are no less spiritual today than they were in the past, but they are a lot less religious – at least, in a formal sense. A disconnect has occurred between religion and spirituality: people no longer see religion or Church as the natural setting in which to explore or express their spiritual aspirations. So they are drifting away from churches in droves. However, they are not doing so because they no longer believe in God, or because they have no hunger or interest in the spiritual aspect of life, but because, in their experience of Church, they are neither finding a faith they can believe in, nor an existential spirituality that can sustain their souls in an age of anxiety and estrangement. Many people long to reconnect with the sacred mystery of life, to discover their place in the cosmos, but they don't see Church or religion as a way of achieving this.

This book, which originated as talks in St Luke's church in West Holloway, London, where I am the vicar, is written for people both within and beyond the Church who would like to discover a re-enchantment with Christianity, who wish to find fresh ways to think *and* feel about the Christian faith, and who want to go about the business of connecting it with other aspects of their life and experience. I am arguing that for this to happen, two things are necessary: first, we need to identify ways to interpret Christian belief that make sense today; and second, we need some kind of spiritual renewal: re-enchanted faith is Spirited faith.

One of the main causes of disenchantment with Christianity

is the attitude of insularity found in many churches where Christian faith exists in a bubble, virtually uninfluenced by the insights, wisdom and sensibilities of the emerging culture of the twenty-first century. For faith to flourish it must engage in a vigorous conversation both with its own past and with contemporary culture. It is about looking both backwards and forwards. Christian faith must neither amount to a simple repetition of past doctrinal formulations, nor a mere echoing of present attitudes, but be a dialectic between the two.[1]

Some people will say that my re-enchanted version of Christianity is simply a liberal interpretation. However, I am neither interested in being 'liberal' nor 'conservative'. These are threadbare categories from the past. My interest lies in finding expressions of Christianity that are both rooted in the originating sources of the Christian faith and which also make sense to people today. I prefer, therefore, to describe myself as progressive orthodox, a term I shall describe in Chapter 3. Basically, there are two kinds of Christianity, the first of which insists that divine revelation is an entirely past event, while the other affirms that there are always new things to learn. I would argue that the first approach is not only mistaken, but also unbiblical. Jesus himself said that there were many things yet to be revealed that he was unable to share, but that the Spirit would lead us into all the truth (John 16.12–13). A progressive approach to revelation is not only permitted but also required by Christ's own vision of the work of the Holy Spirit.

We live in an extraordinary time in the Western world, when church attendances are diminishing but spiritual hunger is rising. This book is a response to the challenge of this situation, which is articulated so evocatively by David Tacey in his inspiring book *The Spirituality Revolution*:

How ironic if the ball of Western civilization is now back in the religious court, but the court of religion does not know about it, or has stopped playing ball with the world. What if it ignores the present challenge or does not care enough to take up a dialogue with the world? The yearning for sacredness, spiritual meaning, security, and personal engagement with the spirit are the primary needs and longings of the contemporary world. What is happening if the institutions of faith are so bound up with themselves and resistant to change that they cannot make some contribution to these needs? Our contemporary situation is full of ironies and paradoxes. Chief among these is that our secular society has given birth to a sense of the sacred, and yet our sacred traditions are failing to recognize the spiritual potential.[2]

Dave Tomlinson
dave@davetomlinson.co.uk
www.davetomlinson.co.uk

Notes

1 For a stimulating discussion of this dialectic, see Andrew Linzey, 'On Theology', in Paul A. B. Clarke, Andrew Linzey and John Moses (eds), *Theology, The University and the Modern World*, London: Lester Crook Academic Publishing, 1988, pp. 29–66.
2 David Tacey, *The Spirituality Revolution: The Emergence of Contemporary Spirituality*, Hove: Brunner-Routledge, 2004, p. 20.

Behind the Mask of Certainty

Is re-enchantment possible?

The ancient Hopi people of North America have a fascinating rite of passage for their children as they move into young adulthood. Throughout their life these children have been familiar with the Kachinas, the tribe's masked holy men, who bless the corn harvest and bring toys and gifts for the children, like Santa Claus. But one night as the children are brought to the sacred circle, something different occurs: on this occasion, instead of giving them gifts, the Kachinas simply remove their masks, revealing the fact that these figures whom the children thought were gods are actually their family and neighbours – people whom they see every day. It is a moment of sacred disenchantment, when childish naivety gives way to grown-up reality.

Sadly, the Church offers no equivalent of the Hopi ritual; there is no 'Service of Disenchantment' to help us figure out what are the 'childish things' about Christianity that should be left behind, and what are the things we need to hold on to. For churchgoers the process is much more messy and fraught – yet essential. Indeed, paradoxically, experiencing disenchantment with the Christian faith is actually fundamental to growing as a Christian. It is the reality check that brings into question all that we have simply taken for granted, the acid bath that purges naive assumptions, false religious pretensions and unthinking conformity.

But what lies beyond the disenchantment? What do we do when the mask is removed and we realize that things cannot be the way they were – or the way we thought they were? That is what this book is about. One thing is clear: once the mask is removed it can never be put back in place – the original innocence is gone, never to be restored. Does this mean that we are damned to eternal cynicism, an everlasting cycle of doubt and suspicion? Or is there a second innocence: a means of re-enchantment? Can we still continue journeying confidently with the Christian faith while also entertaining serious doubts and questions?

When the young Hopi sees for the first time the face behind the mask, he or she must face a decision: to treat the whole world of religion as a charade, a sick joke, or to move forward to a more adult reality in the rituals and symbols of their people, a reality that points to a deeper mystery.

In 1 Corinthians 13, St Paul points to a deeper mystery within Christianity, which we cannot fully encounter in this life. What we experience now, he says, is like a poor reflection in a mirror, or an enigmatic riddle. To pursue this deeper mystery through the riddles and symbols of the Christian faith, knowing that they themselves are not that mystery, is to follow the path towards a second innocence, a point of re-enchantment.

Yet it is painfully clear that lots of people don't make it through to a second innocence of faith: we are surrounded by people who used to believe, who used to go to church, but no longer do. Often, it is because they are locked into interpretations of Christianity that they can no longer own or accept. This is very sad, since, in truth, Christian tradition is so wonderfully rich and diverse: there are always other interpretations, other ways of looking at issues, other spiritual paths to explore, if only we know how to find them.

The assumption is often made that those who struggle with doubts and questions, those who drift away from the Church or even from mainstream Christianity, are in some way spiritually substandard; that they lack the grit or piety to pursue the Christian faith. Yet the reality is quite often the reverse: it is the doubters, the people who have outgrown the hand-me-downs of religious certainty yet who continue to ask the questions, who are on a genuine faith journey.

'When I was a child,' St Paul says, 'I spoke like a child, I thought like a child, I reasoned like a child; when I became an adult, I put an end to childish ways' (1 Cor. 13.11). We are not meant to remain the same, to stick with the same outlook on life or to hang on to the same old beliefs and attitudes, come what may. We are meant to grow as people, and as that growth occurs all kinds of changes will come about in the way we go about interpreting and applying our Christian faith. This can be exciting and stimulating, but it can also be unnerving – both to ourselves and, more especially, to those around us.

For more than twenty years now, the phenomenon of the changing stages of faith has been recognized and studied in various ways. James Fowler, the most influential theorist in the field, has mapped out seven distinct stages that can occur in a person's faith development. He suggests that, as this happens, significant changes are likely to occur in:

1 the way people think;
2 their ability to see another's point of view;
3 the way they arrive at moral judgements;
4 the way and extent to which they draw boundaries around their faith community;
5 the way they relate to external 'authorities' and their truth-claims;
6 the way they form their world-view; and
7 the way they understand and respond to religious symbols.[1]

Clearly, the content and form of a person's faith will indeed change as he or she progresses through these changes of outlook – even, perhaps, to the point of seeming to disappear at times. Yet each stage of faith is, in its own right, fully part of the Christian experience.

The psychotherapist M. Scott Peck, who offers a simplified version of Fowler's stages of faith, makes the fascinating observation that, if people who were religious came to him in pain and trouble, and if they became engaged in the therapeutic process, they frequently left therapy as sceptics, agnostics or even atheists. On the other hand, if atheists, agnostics or sceptics came in similar circumstances and underwent therapy, they frequently left the process as deeply religious people. This puzzled Peck: 'Same therapy, same therapist, successful but utterly different outcomes from a religious point of view.' It didn't make sense, he says, until he realized that 'we are not all in the same place spiritually.'[2] Spiritual growth can mean quite different things to different people at different stages in their life.

There is a stage, perhaps many stages, in life when disenchantment, a process of deconstructing one's faith, is an essential element in spiritual growth. Far from being the end of faith, this simply signals one's need of a deeper and more real encounter with God born out of personal experience instead of unthinking conformity. Sadly, however, this is not the way the process is viewed in lots of churches, where spiritual growth and maturity are equated with ever more fervent affirmations of the Church's teachings, rather than with an honest quest for truth and spiritual reality.

This begs the question: are churches supposed to be gatherings of like-minded believers who all share the same views on the Holy Trinity, salvation, the priesthood, sexuality, the infallibility of scripture and the meaning of the ten-horned beast in Revelation? Or should they, as I believe, be communities of openness and diversity, where sceptics, doubters and dissenters are as welcome as those who appear perfectly settled with the tenets of their faith?

For many of us, the Christian faith is fraught with complex questions to which there cannot be one single, straightforward explanation: questions about the very nature of God, about the person of Jesus, about the Bible, the Church, social ethics, and many other issues. For sure, one does not need a PhD to be a Christian, but when people wake up to the realization that faith is not so simple as they were led to believe, they frequently end up walking away, disillusioned.

Over the past ten years or so I have had frequent visits from students studying theology, many of whom come from conservative churches. Each of their stories has a similar ring: nothing had prepared them for the onslaught their faith received in the first term at college or university. Like the Hopi who are suddenly exposed to what lies behind the masks, they realize that nothing can ever be the same again. One young man I talked with recently says that there is no way he can return to his home church, let alone pursue the ministry he once thought he would discover. He is leaving college with his degree later this year, but will now seek a very different path in life, which probably won't include going to church. And one young woman told me that her home group were praying against the spirit of liberalism in her college – a conservative evangelical Bible college!

The gap between critical approaches to Christianity and the simplistic spirituality promoted in lots of churches lies at the heart of so much disillusionment with Christianity today. Many long for an expression of the Christian faith that reconciles heart and head, that offers a positive, engaging spirituality which is also committed to grappling honestly with difficult and painful questions, and which longs to make the world a better place.

Is re-enchantment with Christianity possible? Having deconstructed our simplistic notions of faith, having committed ourselves to the critical path and seen behind the 'mask', can we discover a second innocence? I believe so. However, this re-enchantment is not a return to credulity, a recapturing of some previous *en*chantment with Christianity. Rather, it is the realization that, when the processes of doubt and deconstruction have run their course, a deeper mystery still waits to be explored and encountered. After wading through the mire of religious nonsense encountered in some churches, this realization can come as both a surprise and a great relief, as a letter I received in response to *The Post-Evangelical* colourfully illustrates:

A year ago I was in a state of rage bordering on church burning. I felt like Winston having escaped from Big Brother or the savage in *Brave New World*, and wanted revenge for all those miserable-worm guilt feelings, and the ludicrous new-speak that had been my life for twenty years. There was no church I could go into without having a severe reaction and either walking out or putting my fingers in my ears and going 'la la la la' – which my wife found embarrassing and looked like demonization to those who are so wise about these things ... A copy of your book and a visit to Greenbelt were the first indications that I was not entirely alone. I am now completely free from that stifling kind of religion that slowly strangles the life out of you and from the susceptibility to completely flee reality. My spirituality is now my own, not an undigested mixture introjected from a thousand grim sermons and silly books. I can get in touch with the strength of it, deep inside. I can read the words of Jesus, but their meaning has now changed like rain into snowflakes. My mind is now open and not tight shut, and I feel an almost primitive sense of freedom and energy.

Re-enchantment involves discovering expressions of faith and spirituality that one can own for oneself. This doesn't mean reinventing Christianity but finding ways to inhabit it that feel authentic and credible. Without this, the faith journey will be frustrating, and possibly short-lived.

This book is a primer in re-enchantment. It isn't a systematic theology or a definitive statement of re-enchanted Christianity, but rather notes from a journey: thoughts and experiences from one who is still travelling the path of re-enchantment. The key is to remain both critical *and* receptive. All too frequently these are mutually exclusive attitudes in church circles, with receptivity resulting in an absence of critical factors, and criticism ruling out receptivity.

Madeleine L'Engle seems to get it about right when she writes:

If my religion is true, it will stand up to all my questioning; there is no need to fear. But if it is not true, if it is man's imposing strictures on God (as did the men of the Christian establishment of Galileo's day) then I want to be open to God, not to what men say about God. I want to be open to revelation, to new life, to new birth, to new light.[3]

Notes

1 James Fowler, *Stages of Faith*, New York: Harper & Row, 1981.

2 M. Scott Peck, *The Different Drum*, London: Arrow Books, 1990, p. 188.

3 Madeleine L'Engle, *Glimpses of Grace*, New York: HarperCollins, 1998, p. 28.

2

Second Innocence

How to be 'called again'

Pat and I have recently renewed a friendship with someone we had lost contact with many years ago. We first met Mike in the early 1970s, when he was a zealous young convert, enthusiastic to tell the world about Jesus. He had long blond hair, an infectious smile and a hippy shoulder bag bulging with tracts and Jesus stickers. At the time, Mike was living in a Christian community whose main aim was to spread the word through preaching and music. Despite its trendy garb, the community's theology was fundamentalist. For a while this suited Mike, but within a couple of years, doubts and questions arose in his mind, some of which were linked directly to his struggle to reconcile Christianity with his being homosexual. When he found no way of squaring the two, he left the community, his faith severely dented.

When we bumped into Mike from time to time over the years, it was apparent that he felt alienated from the Church, but we never really talked about it. Then, a couple of years ago, after a long spell during which we had not seen him, Mike contacted us and came around for dinner. We exchanged stories and talked about the way our faith had changed over the years. Mike was clearly looking to reconstruct his faith, but wasn't sure how. The next day I received an email in which he wrote: 'I shudder as I look back on my fundamentalist days. But here I am now, a 53-year-old gay man, wondering if I can recover some of the passion I once felt about Jesus. Our conversation has left me feeling that maybe I can.'

The story is not uncommon: many people who are disaffected with the church and certain forms of Christianity still long to discover a faith that they can inhabit with honesty and integrity.

During the 1990s Pat and I led a group called Holy Joes, whose entire *raison d'être* was to cater for people like Mike. For ten years in a pub in South London we listened over many pints of beer to unremitting stories of anger, hurt, disappointment and confusion – mopping up plenty of tears into the bargain.

Holy Joes was, for many, a last-chance saloon, a final throw of the dice before walking away from the Church – and possibly from Christianity too. Most of those who came were in their twenties or early thirties, a few (like me) were a little older; some were pushy and hard to shut up, others were content to sit and listen; some wanted heady discussion, others needed somewhere to vent their spleen. What Holy Joes offered was a 'no holds barred' opportunity to discuss, debate and argue about whatever it was with the church and Christianity that got their goat. No one passed judgement on what was heard or seen. There were no 'right' answers imposed at the end of the evening. For some, it really did prove to be a last stopping off point before leaving the Church (for the time being, at any rate), but for lots of others it turned out to be the much-needed incentive to keep on journeying, and even a stepping-stone back into church life.

Perhaps the greatest virtue of Holy Joes was the refusal to treat people as backsliders simply because they had doubts, or because they were angry or hurt, or because they found church boring, or because they didn't want to 'worship', or because they sometimes felt like throwing a hymn book at the preacher. Indeed, the assumption was that it would be strange if we didn't feel such things at times.

On the face of it, St Luke's, where I am now the vicar, is a more conventional style of church, but actually it offers a quite similar environment to Holy Joes: an inclusive community where people of all stages of faith and none can embark with integrity on a voyage of discovery, searching perhaps for a second innocence, for a new way to reconnect with the heart of Christianity.

I first came across the idea of a second innocence in the writings of the French philosopher Paul Ricoeur, who died in 2005. Ricoeur is renowned for his work in the field of hermeneutics: the theory of interpretation. He was a man of faith who grew up in a devout Protestant background in Catholic France. And while most of his work was not specifically religious, he made a major contribution to an understanding of how to interpret the texts and symbols of Christianity. He has been described as the 'hermeneutical equivalent of John the Baptist',[1] that is, his approach prepares the way for new and liberating ways to interpret the texts and symbols of Christianity today. That said, his work is aimed at the philosophical specialist, so it isn't bedtime reading for most of us.

One of Ricoeur's most famous creations is the 'hermeneutical arc', a three-step methodology to plot a dialectic movement (thesis – antithesis – synthesis) in the interpretation of a text. According to this, reading starts with a naive acceptance of the text and its literal sense. This is followed by a moment of disenchantment when a critical distance appears between reader and text and truthfulness, when intellectual honesty and objectivity come to the fore. Finally, Ricoeur's arc suggests the possibility of a 'second naiveté': a moment of reconnection with the text, which in no way bypasses criticism, but rather moves *through* it to attain a new understanding. Ricoeur also called this third stage a 'postcritical' moment.[2]

Ricoeur's notion of a 'second naiveté' has countless applications, not least in shedding light on the changing patterns of the spiritual journey. For most of us, that journey starts with a wide-eyed acceptance of the Christian message as it is presented to us. Following this, at some stage we encounter doubts and questions that generate a critical distance from the faith we once embraced, threatening its entire credibility in our minds. Finally, a new understanding emerges that is deeper and more mature, which is informed and sharpened by the doubts and questions. So we eventually discover a faith that is a synthesis of belief and doubt – a second innocence.

Sadly, however, many people do not progress beyond the second stage in the process, the deconstruction of faith. Having experienced disenchantment, having seen behind the mask of religious certainty, they then presume that there is nowhere else to go in terms of faith development. So the journey comes to an end.

Perhaps part of the difficulty is that the only apparent choice available to doubters and sceptics is either to return to their original 'naiveté' or to abandon faith altogether. In reality, the first option has disappeared: once the questions have been acknowledged, the doubts expressed, the critical process embraced, there is no going back. Something of the immediacy of belief, the sense of certainty, has been lost and cannot be recovered. So the only available course appears to be that of leaving faith behind. However, re-enchantment is achievable: an aspiration voiced in Ricoeur's magnificent heart-cry: 'Beyond the desert of criticism, we wish to be called again.'

So how does a second innocence come about? How do we reconnect with the Christian faith once we have entertained doubts and questions? How can we be 'called again'? Ricoeur is very clear: 'It is by *interpreting* that we can *hear* again.' Vibrant faith and spirituality can be rediscovered only by entering the matrix of interpretation, by grappling with the paradoxes of an ancient tradition and by engaging imaginatively with contemporary insights and understanding.

In some parts of the Church the whole process of reinterpretation is seen as rather unnecessary and futile. For such people, the truth is clear and unambiguous, and must be taken simply at face value. But for the rest of us, things are just not that straightforward.

To begin with, we are children of a *scientific age*. We cannot take at face value, therefore, an ancient text that tells us that the world was created in six days, when we understand that it evolved over billions of years. But more than that, the scientific outlook has led us to doubt and question what we are told as a matter of course – even when we are reading the Bible. This leaves Christians much to contemplate: is the Bible true, or in what sense is it true? What about the creation accounts in Genesis, and stories like Noah and the ark, the crossing of the Red Sea, or Jonah being swallowed by a big fish? More importantly, what do we make of the doctrine of the incarnation, the virgin birth, the miracle accounts in the Gospels or the resurrection and ascension of Christ?

Yet, essentially, there is no intrinsic conflict between science and faith, once we are willing to place our faith into the matrix of interpretation. The real question is not, 'Do we believe the Bible?', but 'How do we interpret the Bible in order to make sense of it in a scientific age?' And as we grapple with that question, others follow hot on its heels. How do we make sense of the credal faith of the early Church that was formulated in an entirely different cultural context from our own? How can we glean the wisdom of ancient ideas in a scientific age? Can we reconcile present-day ethics of equality with texts that appear prejudiced against women, gay people and others? In short, what do the antiquated texts, symbols and rituals of Christianity offer to the world of the twenty-first century?

We are also members of a *pluralist society* that recognizes the value of cultural and religious diversity. Living, as we do, in a community where difference is not only taken for granted but celebrated, requires us to re-examine and reinterpret aspects of our faith. And so another bunch of questions surfaces: How does God look upon people of other faiths? Is God bigger than Christianity? Are we supposed to get people to change their religion and join us, or can we accept that they are being led by God along a different route? Is there still a role for Christian mission in a pluralist world, and if so, what should it be?

Then there are questions that arise from living in a *global community* in which we are aware as never before of injustice, inequality and oppression in places near and far. In the past, missionaries were sent to 'lands of darkness' to convert the heathen to Christianity. But now we recognize the darkness in our own land and in the western world in general, where a massive edifice of economic progress is built on a legacy of trade injustice. Many people leave the Church or become disillusioned with Christianity because they see little sign that justice is a priority. Charities and campaigning groups that actively pursue a more just and equitable world are littered with people who used to go to church, who used to believe and now practise some form of churchless spirituality. The faith of such people could only be re-enchanted through a radical reinterpretation of the priorities of Christian faith and mission.

Nicholas Lash, a former Professor of Divinity at Cambridge University and author of many books, argues that the confusion and uncertainty which many Christians experience today is perhaps less obviously the expression of a crisis of faith than a crisis of culture: 'We are not sure how to go about the business of *connecting* our Christianity with other aspects of our life and experience.'[3]

This was precisely where our friend Mike's disenchantment with Christianity arose: much as he wanted to believe, he just couldn't make the connection between his faith and his experience in the rest of life. But the real problem lay in the narrowness of the Christian tradition to which he had been exposed. And he is not alone: countless people walk away from Christianity because they are unaware of the vastly different interpretations of Christianity that are available to them.

Finally, before moving on, I should stress that a second innocence is simply another point on a journey, not the destination. Ricoeur's hermeneutical arc actually turns out to be a circle that must be re-entered constantly. So there is no final configuration, no definitive interpretation that excludes other considerations, other possibilities. Second innocence is a synthesis of belief and doubt. The American writer, Frederick Buechner, reflects: 'If you don't have doubts, you are either kidding yourself or are asleep.'[4] I would add: if you don't have doubts, you actually don't have faith, you have certainty, which is quite a different thing.

Notes

1 Kevin J. Vanhoozer, 'The Joy of Yes: Ricoeur: Philosopher of Hope', in *The Christian Century*, Vol. 122, 23 August 2005.

2 Paul Ricoeur, *The Symbolism of Evil*, Boston: Beacon Press, 1967, pp. 347–57.

3 Nicholas Lash, *Theology on Dover Beach*, London: Darton, Longman & Todd, 1979, p. ix.

4 Frederick Buechner, *Beyond Words*, New York: HarperCollins, 2004, p. 85.

3

Progressive Orthodoxy

'You have to change to stay the same'

How do we go about connecting our Christian faith with other aspects of our life and experience? This is a dilemma that every Christian faces at some point. What do we do when values and attitudes now taken for granted in society seem to conflict with the assumed teachings of the Bible or the traditions of the Church? This is precisely the question behind, for example, the current heated discussion in the Church about homosexuality, and women priests and bishops. But it's also the question behind the evolution versus creationism argument, or behind disputes over stem-cell research, or abortion – or even whether Christians can practise yoga! It is about a clash of cultures, a conflict of authorities. Those on the 'conservative' side of the arguments believe that Christian identity is under attack from a liberal, secular agenda, while 'progressives' feel that Christianity needs rescuing from those who want to lock it into the past.

The problem centres on what we think the historical character of Christian faith and theology to be. Christianity is a historical religion; no one can dispute this, but what does the phrase 'historical religion' mean? Maurice Wiles, the former Regius Professor of Divinity at Oxford University, observes that 'historical' can be understood in two ways. On the one hand, it might mean that Christian tradition is fixed, that we can't mess with it, that we are bound by the character, language or content of its origins: 'We are tied to the past.' Alternatively, 'historical' could mean that Christianity is part of the changing patterns of history; that it is prepared to adapt itself to changing circumstances, and that making such changes will actually ensure its continuity and vitality.[1]

But are we faced with an absolute choice between these two explanations?[2] Personally, I wish to maintain that Christianity is an historical religion in both senses of the phrase – that the Christian faith is indeed radically dependent on the past, on particular historical events, but that it is also a living, evolving faith that must adapt to new situations, new circumstances, new insights. As Archbishop Robert Runcie once said: 'A church which listens only to its tradition will end up speaking only to itself. A church which listens only to what is happening in the world will end up becoming only a dull echo of the latest liberal fashion. It is the interplay between tradition and discovery that creates a proper relevance.'[3]

My own way of describing this third way of thinking about Christianity is to label it 'progressive orthodoxy' – a faith that is fed and nurtured by a rootedness in past events (the 'orthodox' bit), but which is also shaped and energized by a dynamic interaction with the world of the present (the 'progressive' bit). Some people will object even to this use of the term 'orthodox' on the grounds that the word inevitably smacks of rigidity and inflexibility; that it is intrinsically backward-looking. But this need not necessarily be the case. And I am personally disinclined to hand the term over to those who are indeed rigid and inflexible about Christianity.

In an essay written some years ago, Rowan Williams identified two distinctly different approaches to the term 'orthodoxy'[4]. The first is a closed system. It is pre-packed, predetermined, watertight, a comprehensive ideology. This sort of orthodoxy stifles thought and distorts perception. It allows no real conversation. It is a monologue. No critical element is admitted. The reason that there is no conversation in this kind of orthodoxy is because actually everything has already been said, and all that is left to do is repeat it again and again *ad nauseam*. There can be nothing new to say that isn't just a reiteration in different ways of what has already been said.

The second approach to orthodoxy is basically what I am

calling 'progressive orthodoxy'. Here, orthodoxy is seen, not as pre-packed truth handed down from the past, but as a tradition of shared speech, of shared symbols, a living community of revelation and dialogue, a tradition that invites a process of critical questioning. This approach to orthodoxy does not claim to possess the truth, simply to have perspectives on truth. Tradition is not static and fixed, but dynamic and evolving. Progressive orthodoxy centres on a dialogue between the traditions of the past and the insights and struggles of now. It affirms that there are always new things to see and understand; that divine revelation is a constant process and not a once-and-for-all event in the past.[5]

In its own pink and fluffy way, the film *My Big Fat Greek Wedding* is all about the tension between tradition and progress. Toula, the central figure, clashes with her traditional Greek father when she falls in love with a non-Greek whom she wants to marry. She desperately wants to please her father, but can't give up her new love. In a moment of anguish, she pours out her heart to her brother Nick, who drops an unexpected pearl of wisdom, saying: 'Toula, don't let your past dictate who you are, but let it be part of who you will become.' Could this gem of popular cinematography perhaps offer a working definition of progressive orthodoxy – a faith that is deeply rooted in the originating sources of Christianity but which recognizes that the Holy Spirit continues to reveal new insights in the present situation?

Those who follow the first approach to orthodoxy believe that their rigid conservatism is an act of faithfulness to the gospel. I disagree. Being faithful to the gospel does not suggest preserving it in precisely the same form that it was originally given. Rather, it entails reconfiguring and reinterpreting the message in order that it can connect with new situations that are culturally and historically quite different from the original setting. Maggi Dawn, Chaplain and Fellow of Robinson College, Cambridge University, encapsulates the point perfectly with her pithy remark: 'We have to change to stay the same.' In other words, 'In order to stay in continuity with Christian tradition, we must also engage with the radical discontinuity of cultural expression. Meaning is not fixed, and if our religious language does not change, then far from maintaining continuity, it actually takes us away from the heart of the Christian tradition.'[6] In a similar vein, Thomas Merton, the acclaimed Catholic spiritual writer and poet, writes that to cling to the past is actually to lose one's continuity with the past, 'since this means clinging to what is no longer there'.[7]

'Progressive orthodoxy' may be a new label, but the idea is far from new. Indeed, this is how Christian tradition has always worked. As John V. Taylor, the English bishop and theologian, observes, the story of Christianity has been, and always will be, a series of impromptu responses to events. 'A religion, like every other system of ideas or body of tradition, stands in a context of exchange, affecting and being affected by its historical and social situation. This truth is implicit in the biblical understanding of revelation.' There are many who firmly deny that this is so, Taylor concedes: 'To such Christians religion is a self-contained subculture, pursuing an autonomous belief-system and way of life derived from a divine revelation and, consequently, independent of the history of a world which impinges only inasmuch as it promotes or restricts religious freedom.' However, 'historical investigation lends little support to the notion that influence can be confined to a one-way flow'.[8] Meaning can never be fixed, and any revelation which is mediated through human thought, language and experience (which, according to Christian belief, divine revelation certainly is), 'must also then be historically contingent, sociologically embedded and linguistically specific'.

Richard Hooker, the sixteenth-century architect of Anglicanism, marked out the ground for a progressive orthodoxy with his 'three-legged stool' – the notion that Christian truth exists in the interaction of scripture, tradition and reason, and that none of these can be properly understood without the others. In 1988, the Lambeth Conference decided that a fourth leg should be added: the experience of God's people. The biblical text, of course, remains constant, but reason and experience are continually changing, and tradition evolves out of the interaction between the text and contemporary expressions of reason and experience.

Christian orthodoxy, then, should not be understood as some fixed body of doctrinal or moral teaching, or as a rigid pattern of ritual or liturgy, but as a conversation between past and present, between scripture and reason, between tradition and experience.

Tradition itself is and always has been a conversation, a dialogue – an argument, even. The Christian movement has always embodied conflicting points of view, always included debate, dispute and disagreement. Christian tradition is, to borrow a phrase from Paul Ricoeur, a 'conflict of interpretations'. In contrast to this, the fundamentalist impulse is to forestall discussion, to exclude other perspectives, to bring premature closure to the argument by insisting that the fundamentalist view alone represents the authentic voice of Christian truth.

Yet, in the final analysis, the priority of the gospel lies not with textual debates and arguments, with the internal squabbling of conservatives and progressives, but with the liberation of human beings to be the whole persons that they might be: spiritually, physically, psychologically, emotionally and socially. And the Church's faithfulness to its message and tradition must ultimately be tested in terms of how effectively it helps to bring about that freedom.

The Bible is at the very centre of Christian tradition, and throughout history the Bible has often been the catalyst of human liberation. In the year 380, for instance, it inspired Gregory of Nyssa to condemn slavery. In the nineteenth century it led evangelical believers to help bring about the abolition of the slave trade. It has led Christians to fight poverty and injustice, to contend for greater equality of the sexes. And in our own day it has inspired movements for justice, fair trade, peace, and care for creation. Yet the Bible has also been a tool of tyranny and devastation. For 1,400 years it was used to portray Africans as cursed by God, and to justify their enslavement. It was used to sanction medieval witch-hunts. Perverse biblical interpretation was employed to justify apartheid. It is still used to exclude women from ministry and leadership in the Church, to oppress gay people and to destroy the environment. Clearly, the Bible can be used and abused in many different ways in order to serve many different agendas.

The vast gulf between biblical times and our own time causes many to treat the Bible as nothing more than a classical text, a piece of history that has undoubtedly helped to shape Western culture, but which has no real relevance for us today. I certainly reject that view. Like Ricoeur, I want to be 'called again'. I want to be receptive to God's Spirit mediated, albeit messily, through the oddity and ambiguity of this ancient text. 'It is by *interpreting* that we can *hear* again.'

I have devoted the past twenty years of my ministry to getting people involved in the process of reinterpreting the Christian message: goading them into sharing their doubts and questions, encouraging them to join the arguments, to share their ideas, insights and experiences, and helping them to recognize that they can be part of creating Christian tradition rather than feeling that they are its victims.

Kenneth Burke, the literary theorist and philosopher, describes the drama of history as an 'unending conversation'. His portrayal could equally apply to Christian tradition:

Where does the drama of history get its material? From the 'unending conversation' that is going on at the point in history when we were born. Imagine that you enter a parlour. You come late. When you arrive, others have long preceded you, and they are engaged in a heated discussion, a discussion too heated for them to pause and tell you exactly what it is about. In fact, the discussion had already begun long before any of them got there, so that no one present is qualified to retrace for you all the steps that had gone before. You listen for a while; then you put in your oar. Someone answers; you answer him; another comes to your defence; another aligns himself against you, to either the embarrassment or gratification of your opponent, depending upon the quality of your ally's assistance. However, the discussion is interminable. The hour grows late, you must depart. And you do depart, with the discussion still vigorously in progress.[9]

Progressive orthodoxy affirms the importance of Christianity's past: of the events and sacred texts that have given it shape and form and content; but it also maintains the imperative for Christianity to change and evolve through a constructive *and* critical engagement with the progressive movements of history. In order to remain faithful to its originating sources, Christian tradition must develop and change, by engaging in a vigorous conversation between sources and memories from the past, experiences and insights from the present, and hopes and visions from the future. You are invited to be a part of this conversation.

Notes

1 M. F. Wiles, 'In What Sense is Christianity a "Historical" Religion?', in *Explorations in Theology*, 4, London, 1979, p. 53.

2 Nicholas Lash argues the pros and cons of Maurice Wiles' two definitions of 'historical' in *Theology on Dover Beach*, London: Darton, Longman & Todd, 1979, pp. xi–xix.

3 R. Runcie, 'Theology, the University and the Modern World', in Paul A. B. Clarke, Andrew Linzey and John Moses (eds), *Theology, the University and the Modern World*, London: Lester Crook Academic Publishing, 1988, p. 26.

4 R. Williams, 'What is Catholic Orthodoxy?', in Kenneth Leech and Rowan Williams (eds), *Essays Catholic and Radical*, London: The Bowerdean Press, 1983, pp. 11–25.

5 My description of the two approaches to orthodoxy owes much to Kenneth Leech's comments on Rowan Williams' essay in his excellent book, *Subversive Orthodoxy: Traditional Faith and Radical Commitment*, Toronto: Anglican Book Centre, 1992, p. 49f.

6 Maggi Dawn, 'You Have to Change to Stay the Same', in Cray et al. (eds), *The Post-Evangelical Debate*, London: SPCK, 1997, pp. 35–56.

7 Thomas Merton, *A Vow of Conversation: Journals 1964–1965*, New York: Farrar, Straus & Giroux, 1988, p. 19.

8 J. Taylor, 'The Future of Christianity', in John McManners (ed.), *The Oxford Illustrated History of Christianity*, Oxford: Oxford University Press, 1992, p. 628.

9 Quoted in M. Borg, *The Heart of Christianity: Rediscovering a Life of Faith*, New York: HarperCollins, 2003, p. 19.

4

The Good Book Guide

It's by interpreting that we can believe again

In short, one way to describe the Bible, written by many different people over a period of three thousand years and more, would be to say that it is a disorderly collection of sixty-odd books, which are often tedious, barbaric and obscure, and which teem with contradictions and inconsistencies. It is a swarming compost of a book, an Irish stew of poetry and propaganda, law and legalism, myth and murk, history and hysteria. Over the centuries it has become hopelessly associated with tub-thumping evangelism and dreary piety, with superannuated superstition and blue-nosed moralizing, with ecclesiastical authoritarianism and crippling literalism.[1]

Frederick Buechner's portrayal of the Bible could probably get him lynched in some churches. He certainly isn't a fundamentalist! Yet anyone familiar with his writings knows that Buechner is a dedicated and enlightening teacher of scripture, who on the one hand affirms the Bible as God's Word, yet on the other recognizes it as a deeply human work. There are many reasons not to read the Bible, Buechner says: the barbarities, the often fanatical nationalism, the passages where God is interested in other nations only to the degree that he can use them to whip Israel into line, the self-righteousness and self-pity of many of the Psalms, God hardening Pharaoh's heart only to then clobber him for his hard-heartedness, and so on.[2] Yet Buechner continues to read the Bible, clearly receptive to its message but ever aware of the limitations and prejudices of its writers.

The path to re-enchantment with the Bible begins with an

unambiguous acknowledgement that there are historical, scientific and ethical difficulties with the text which cannot be ignored or bypassed. But it also requires that the text be read with receptiveness, rooted in the realization that truth and wisdom transcend the categories of modern scientific and historical fact. In other words, in order to hear what the Bible has to say, we must read it both *critically* and *receptively*.

My own relationship with the Bible could certainly be defined by these two elements. Over the years I have variously loved the Bible and hated it, listened to it and ignored it, been irritated by it and captivated by it. I have sometimes felt like throwing it away, sometimes found it impossible to put down. It is, for me, both an intimate friend and a total stranger, a source of immense inspiration and the cause of constant annoyance. It is a push–pull relationship: whenever I try to walk away from the Bible, I find myself inescapably drawn back into it. I am repelled by many sentiments expressed in its pages and by some of its portrayals of God, yet it also inspires and informs my highest and most treasured visions of who God is. And in a curious way it calls me, constantly, to be a better person than I am.

Re-enchantment with the Bible hinges on the discovery of a creative tension between criticism and receptiveness. But sadly, many people fail to discover that creative tension, perhaps because they imagine that it is an all-or-nothing issue: you either accept the Bible as being infallible, as literally true, or you don't. Some people, therefore, choose to ignore the difficulties and simply repeat the mantra of biblical infallibility, while others walk away from the Bible – and from Christianity as well – because they cannot set aside the critical questions.

The absurdity of a literal reading of the Bible was highlighted in an anonymous letter posted on the internet some years ago. It was addressed to Laura Schlessinger, an American radio host who condemned same-sex relationships on her show *Dr Laura*. At the time, Laura Schlessinger was an Orthodox Jew, and she apparently denounced homosexuality from a passage in Leviticus. The unidentified correspondent wrote:

Dear Dr Laura,

Thank you for doing so much to educate people regarding God's Law. I have learned a great deal from your show, and I try to share that knowledge with as many people as I can. When someone tries to defend the homosexual lifestyle, for example, I simply remind them that Leviticus 18.22 clearly states it to be an abomination. End of debate. I do need some advice from you, however, regarding some of the specific laws and how to follow them.

a) When I burn a bull on the altar as a sacrifice, I know it creates a pleasing odour for the Lord (Lev. 1.9). The problem is my neighbours. They claim the odour is not pleasing to them. Should I smite them?

b) I would like to sell my daughter into slavery, as sanctioned in Exodus 21.7. In this day and age, what do you think would be a fair price for her?

c) I know that I am allowed no contact with a woman while she is in her period of menstrual uncleanness (Lev. 15.19–24). The problem is, how do I tell? I have tried asking, but most women take offence.

d) Leviticus 25.44 states that I may indeed possess slaves, both male and female, provided they are purchased from neighbouring nations. A friend of mine claims that this applies to Mexicans, but not Canadians. Can you clarify? Why can't I own Canadians?

e) I have a neighbour who insists on working on the Sabbath. Exodus 35.2 clearly states he should be put to death. Am I morally obligated to kill him myself?

f) A friend of mine feels that even though eating shellfish is an abomination (Lev. 11.10), it is a lesser abomination than homosexuality. I don't agree. Can you settle this?

g) Leviticus 21.20 states that I may not approach the altar of God if I have a defect in my sight. I have to admit that I wear reading glasses. Does my vision have to be 20/20, or is there some wiggle room here?

h) Most of my male friends get their hair trimmed, including the hair around their temples, even though this is expressly forbidden by Leviticus 19.27. How should they die?

i) I know from Leviticus 11.6–8 that touching the skin of a dead pig makes me unclean, but may I still play football if I wear gloves?

j) My uncle has a farm. He violates Leviticus 19.19 by planting two different crops in the same field, as does his wife by wearing garments made of two different kinds of thread (cotton/polyester blend). He also tends to curse and blaspheme a lot. Is it really necessary that we go to all the trouble of getting the whole town together to stone them? (Lev. 24.10–16) Couldn't we just burn them to death at a private family affair like we do with people who sleep with their in-laws? (Lev. 20.14)

I know you have studied these things extensively, so I am confident you can help. Thank you again for reminding us that God's word is eternal and unchanging.

Your devoted disciple and adoring fan.[3]

The letter is good entertainment value. But it also makes a serious hermeneutical point: literalism makes a laughing stock of the Bible – clearly, no sensible person can believe that God declares a menstruating woman unclean, or commands that disobedient children be stoned to death. Biblical literalism must be dumped if the Bible is to be taken seriously.

Yet, as Paul Ricoeur maintains, criticism need not have the last word: there is a path *in and through* criticism to a 'second naiveté', to a *post*-critical re-enchantment with the text. But how do we achieve it? By interpreting, Ricoeur insists: 'We can only believe by interpreting.'[4] In other words, the 'good book' requires good reading, reading that takes seriously the subtleties of dealing with texts from a different time and culture from our own, and which sets aside any idea of treating it as literally true.

Good reading requires the reader to pay attention to the text, to be open or receptive to what it has to say, but it also demands that the reader asks questions of the text – perhaps hard questions – to exercise what Ricoeur calls a 'hermeneutics of suspicion'. Hermeneutics is the science or art of interpreting texts; a hermeneutic of suspicion suggests that we start by asking who or what the text excludes, who is disadvantaged or damaged by the message, both in the original context of the writer, and in our own context today, and what elements are being omitted or obscured by the text.

An example of necessary suspicion can be seen in the way in which African American slaves refused to accept the authority of biblical teachings and their interpretation when those teachings appeared to validate racial prejudice and oppression. The slave community, as we know, was as faithful to the message of Jesus Christ as any in history. In spite of being persecuted, brutalized and killed, their songs, sermons and testimonies powerfully proclaimed their devotion to Christ. They internalized the biblical stories. God's story was their story. But they were not blind to the impact of some of the Bible's teachings or the influence of human interpreters. Howard Thurman, once the dean of the chapel at Howard University, offers an excellent case in point in a record of what his African American grandmother once said to him:

My regular chore was to do all of the reading for my grandmother – she could neither read nor write ... With a feeling of great temerity I asked her one day why it was that she would not let me read any of the Pauline letters. What she told me I shall never forget. 'During the days of slavery', she said, 'the master's minister would occasionally hold services for the slaves ... Always the white minister used as his text something from Paul. At least three or four times a year he used as a text: "Slaves be obedient to them that are your masters ... as unto Christ." Then he would go on to show how, if we were good and happy slaves, God would bless us. I promised my Maker that if I ever learned to read and if freedom ever came, I would never read that part of the Bible.'[5]

In her own way, this lady practised a hermeneutics of suspicion. The preacher's text was in the Bible. But she contested it. Her perception of God and of divine grace was more compelling and authoritative than the text or its interpretation by the white minister.

In more recent times, feminist theologians who have focused attention on the androcentric and patriarchal assumptions and attitudes in the Bible have also exercised a hermeneutic of suspicion. Without dismissing the Bible as such, they resist any suggestion that God is revealed through texts that limit or denigrate women. Elisabeth Schüssler Fiorenza, for example, argues that 'No biblical text that perpetuates violence against women, children, or "slaves" should be accorded the status of divine revelation if we do not want to turn the God of the Bible into a God of violence.'[6]

During the early twentieth century a similar problem was recognized in relation to modern science. The German theologian Rudolph Bultmann felt that modern people were being turned away from Christianity because the Bible no longer stood up in a scientific age. Bultmann felt that we must demythologize the Bible – strip away its mythical trappings so that its core message could continue to be heard. This also is a hermeneutics of suspicion: a questioning of certain assumptions and presuppositions in the Bible in the light of more recent understanding.

The good reader will not abandon the Bible because it assumes a three-tier universe, or because it reflects a culture in which patriarchy or slave ownership are taken for granted, because these are not the essential message of the Bible. The real purpose of the Bible is to draw us into its narrative quest to know and understand God, and, from a Christian perspective, to encounter the person and teachings of Christ. But it is a human book, written by human beings situated in particular cultural settings at specific points in history; and whatever theory of divine inspiration may be attached to its writing, the fact is that the Bible reflects the limited scientific, historical and social outlook of its writers. A hermeneutics of suspicion is directed at uncovering the humanness and the situated nature of the text. It helps us to overcome the idolatry and dogmatism that attach to literal readings.

Good reading of the Bible begins, then, with an unambiguous acknowledgement of the gulf that exists between our own world and the world of the text. As Walter Brueggemann so aptly puts it, 'We are dealing with a very ancient document that did not have in mind our particular set of issues.'[7] So we cannot expect clear-cut, unambiguous answers to questions and dilemmas of the twenty-first century. The Bible cannot provide a manual with step-by-step instructions on tricky subjects like sexuality, genetic engineering or computers that keep crashing; it makes no comment on equal opportunity legislation or civil partnerships. We may draw on the wisdom of scripture in trying to resolve the complicated issues of the twenty-first century, but we must not look to it for clear-cut answers.

Some people try to bypass the business of interpreting the Bible, claiming that they simply read it and believe it. However, there can be no uninterpreted reading; we all create interpretations of the Bible – liberals, conservatives or whoever. The difference is that good readers – of whatever theological persuasion – know that they are interpreting and take responsibility for their interpretations. The process can never be neutral or unbiased: it is 'inescapably subjective, necessarily provisional, and … inevitably disputatious'.[8] We cannot approach the Bible with a blank mind; we unavoidably bring to it preconceptions, attitudes and assumptions which colour our understanding. This is not a problem: without such starting points we could not enter the matrix of interpretation or make sense of what we read. The subjectivity of the reader only becomes a problem if the reader refuses to acknowledge his or her subjectivity and pretends to read the text in some purely objective fashion.

The object of good reading is clear: to attempt to comprehend what the text might mean for us today. Historical-critical research can help to reconstruct the original setting of the text, but most people's real interest lies in what, if anything, the Bible means in the twenty-first century. This may involve looking for new and different meanings in the text more pertinent to our situation. 'It is self-evident that new circumstances of reading permit us to see what we have not seen in the text heretofore', Brueggemann writes.[9] The Bible may not be expected, for example, to address directly issues such as climate change, industrial waste or CO_2 emissions, yet our experience of the ecological crisis enables us to determine new readings of scripture that are profoundly relevant to our situation. 'Interpretation is not the reiteration of the text. It is rather the movement of the text beyond itself in fresh ways, often ways never offered until this moment of utterance.'[10]

From a Christian point of view, the core message of the Bible is the gospel, the good news of salvation, justice and liberation in Jesus Christ. It is essential, Brueggemann maintains, to recognize the distinction between the gospel and the Bible. And since much of the Bible is filtered through 'a rather heavy-duty patriarchal ideology', the main task of the reader is to distinguish between the liberating love of God at work in scripture and the attitudes and policies that are really 'organized against the gospel'. Commenting on some of the present struggles in the Church, Brueggemann sees it as very scary that, by equating the gospel with the Bible, we get 'a kind of Biblicism that is not noticeably informed by the gospel'. And he makes the observation that, just as Martin Luther King envisaged the arc of history as bent towards justice, so the arc of the gospel is bent towards inclusiveness.[11]

The assumption that the meaning of the Bible remains a fixed entity over time is patently wrong. Within the Bible itself, the text is on the move. This is seen at a fundamental level in the trajectory of interpretation between the Old and New Testaments, where the Christ-event of the New Testament is a clear and radical interpretation of the Old Testament. 'Christianity is dependent upon its successive readings of scripture', Ricoeur says, 'and on its capacity to reconvert this scripture into the living word.' So there is a 'mutation of meaning' even within the Bible[12] – a trajectory of reinterpretation – and the curve of this trajectory is very definitely bent towards justice and inclusion.

The story of Philip preaching to the Ethiopian eunuch is a marker on the trajectory of inclusion. During the early years of the Church it was presumed that the Christian movement was an exclusively Jewish affair. This was an assumption based on many Old Testament scriptures that foster Jewish exclusiveness. But Philip is told to preach to an African, a black man, who is also a eunuch – someone whose presence was barred from the holy place. And Philip baptizes him. The door of the Church begins to open wider.

However, a little later in Acts, Peter becomes the means of blowing the doors of the Church clean away. In a vision or trance, he is commanded to kill and eat animals forbidden by Mosaic Law for Jews to eat. 'No way!' Peter replies, stating in no uncertain terms his refusal to eat 'unclean' meat. His response is soundly based: the Bible forbids the eating of these animals. He is simply obeying scripture. But the voice is resolute: 'What God has made clean, you must not call profane.' For Peter, obeying God meant disobeying the Bible.

But the process does not stop there. Ricoeur argues that the trajectories move beyond the biblical text into the world of the reader, our world. What is finally to be understood, he says, is not the author or the author's presumed intention, nor is it the structures of the text, but rather the world intended beyond the text – the world of the reader.[13] So again, good reading is not simply a reiteration of the text or a replication of previous interpretations – vital though these be – but the appropriation of the core message of the text (the good news of God's liberating love in Christ) in our world today.

Paul's statement in Galatians 3.28 represents a radical, counter-cultural reinterpretation of the Old Testament, a trajectory of justice and inclusion: 'There is no longer Jew or Greek, there is no longer slave or free, there is no longer male and female; for all of you are one in Christ Jesus.' In this declaration, the basic divisions in the ancient world were overcome. But as we follow its trajectory into the foreground of our own world, we might add that in Christ there is neither gay nor straight.

I have defined progressive orthodoxy as a faith that is fed and nurtured by a rootedness in past events, but which is also shaped and energized by a dynamic interaction with the world of the present. A progressive orthodox reading of scripture is one that creates a vigorous dialogue between the biblical text and the present-day world with its insights, needs and spiritual yearnings. To be progressively orthodox is to pursue fervently the trajectory of the gospel and its expression and outworking in our own day.

Frederick Buechner's depiction of the Bible as 'a swarming compost of a book' is in fact very apt. Compost is the decomposing remnants of organic materials that are packed with rich minerals and natural fertilizer, and on one level the Bible is a heap of leftovers, decomposing remnants of an ancient struggle to understand God in ways that were authentic at the time. We can't reconstruct that past, neither should we wish to, yet in our efforts to understand God afresh in our own age, we can benefit from rich theological nutrients and organic spiritual nourishment from the past mediated to us through scripture.

Notes

1 Frederick Buechner, *Beyond Words*, New York: HarperCollins, 2004, p. 43.

2 Buechner, *Beyond Words*, p. 43.

3 See http://en.wikipedia.org/wiki/Laura_Schlessinger.

4 Paul Ricoeur, *The Symbolism of Evil*, Boston: Beacon Press, 1967, p. 352.

5 Quoted from Brian K. Blount, in 'The Last Word on Biblical Authority', in W. Brueggemann, W. C. Placher and B. K. Blount, *Struggling with Scripture*, Louisville: Westminster John Knox Press, 2002, p. 58.

6 Elisabeth Schüssler Fiorenza, *Bread Not Stone: The Challenge of Feminist Biblical Interpretation*, Boston: Beacon Press, 1984, p. 145.

7 Walter Brueggemann, *The Book That Breathes New Life*, Minneapolis: Fortress Press, 2005, p. 37.

8 Brueggemann, *The Book That Breathes*, p. 26.

9 Brueggemann, *The Book That Breathes*, p. 27.

10 Brueggemann, *The Book That Breathes*, p. 28.

11 Walter Brueggemann, 'The Gospel vs Scripture?', in *Witness Magazine*, November 2002.

12 Paul Ricoeur, 'Preface to Bultmann', in Lewis Smudge (ed.), *Essays on Biblical Interpretation*, London: SPCK, 1981, p. 49f.

13 Paul Ricoeur, 'Toward a Hermeneutic of the Idea of Revelation', in Smudge (ed.), *Essays*, p. 100.

5

Is There Anyone There?

Re-enchanting God-talk

One of the most memorable evenings for Holy Joes was the night we went on a field trip to a pub in Greenwich, for an inter-faith dialogue with a group of Pagans.

It all started when Andrew, a member of the Pagan group (known as Philoso-Forum), started attending Holy Joes. Andrew was a well-read individual who, while not being a Christian, probably had a better grasp of Christian theology than most Christians. During the couple of years that he was with us at Holy Joes he made excellent contributions to our discussions, and even led a couple of evenings.

When Andrew floated the idea of a joint meeting between Holy Joes and Philoso-Forum there was initial hesitation from both groups. But eventually these were overcome and we went on to have three fascinating evenings together. The first was at their pub, so Philoso-Forum set the agenda. I was asked to speak for eight minutes on the topic: 'What I don't like about Christianity' (something I did with unsettling ease). Then Andrew reciprocated with, 'What I don't like about Paganism'. The format was a great success, a brilliant model for non-confrontational dialogue, which created an extremely interesting debate.

Afterwards, a woman thanked me for my part in the evening, saying, 'I think you might have given God back to me.' Rosie had grown up in a vicarage but left home at seventeen vowing never to return. 'When I moved out,' she said, 'it was goodbye to my father and goodbye to his God. I hated both of them!' After a pause she continued, 'I don't know if I'm ready to believe again, but tonight has given me hope that it may at least be a possibility.'

Rosie's disenchantment with her father's religion was entirely understandable. The 'God' she experienced at home was a relentless critic: a harsh parent who always expected more of her than she could give, someone who controlled her with feelings of shame and guilt, and who punished her when she got things wrong. To walk away from such a monstrous deity was not only understandable but also essential for Rosie's spiritual, mental and emotional well-being. And as her story demonstrates, agnosticism, or even downright disbelief, can, paradoxically, become a pathway to real faith.

The idea that people sometimes need to experience periods of agnosticism or disbelief as part of a faith journey does not tend to go down well in some churches, where the dominant view is that Christian maturity is equated with becoming more and more certain about the things one believes. Yet every Christian will pass through periods of doubt, of deconstruction and disbelief. These may occur as the result of a natural process of questioning, or they may be triggered by some crisis event like illness, bereavement, or relationship breakdown; or because of tragic events in the wider world that cause great suffering, like an earthquake or a tsunami. Whatever the cause, it is perfectly normal to experience times of disenchantment with faith.

Having said that, the process of going through dark times can be alarming and unnerving – not least because we cannot be sure where the process will end or what will be left of our faith when it is done. Will we, indeed, still have a faith? Will we still believe that God exists? Or will we decide that the whole thing is a sham? Such questions lurk in the back of most people's minds – even in those of the most fervent believers. And sometimes they need to be allowed to come to the surface.

It is essential to understand that belief in God exists across a wide spectrum of different faith positions. We do not all believe in God in the same way. There is a sliding scale, for instance, between a realist and a non-realist understanding of the meaning of God-talk. The underlying issue is whether or not God-talk has a referent. In other words, does the term 'God' point to an actual reality or a being that exists 'out there'? Or is 'God' essentially a human construct, an imaginative construal to express or represent the human need to believe in some reality beyond the purely material level of existence?

The question appears straightforward – do we or do we not believe in God? But it is actually a lot more complicated than that. Many of us, for example, don't wish to place ourselves in either of the two basic categories from which the argument proceeds.

At one extreme is the category of *literal* or *naive realism*. Here, the assumption is that God-talk is literally true; that there is a clear-cut one-for-one correspondence between religious speech and the thing it describes. So God can be described in the same sense that we talk about everyday objects or experiences. This means that when the Bible speaks of God as, say, Father, or King, or when it depicts God as being angry, or rejoicing, the text is simply describing things the way they are. Similarly, when Exodus reports that God spoke with Moses out of a burning bush, or when Luke records that Jesus ascended from the earth and was received into the clouds, these should be taken as actual events that could have been recorded on an MP3 player or filmed on a camcorder.

At the opposite end of the scale stands *non-realism*. This is the belief that God-talk is just that – God *talk*. From this perspective, there is no actual reality behind or beyond words like 'God', 'heaven', 'truth' or 'morality'; religious language has no referent. This doesn't necessarily mean that God-talk should be dispensed with or rejected out of hand; it is possible to have an essentially non-realist outlook and still recognize that religion plays a significant part in human life and experience. However, in a non-realist framework, there can be no claim to absolute truth or fixed values. If there is no religious reality independent of the human mind and imagination, then words like 'truth' and 'morality' have relative meaning.

The non-realist challenge to Christianity – and to religion in general – is essential in deconstructing the literalist assumptions behind an enormous amount of God-talk. Nothing fuels disenchantment with Christianity more effectively than glib religious speech and empty jargon. Nevertheless, many of us who recoil from vacuous God-talk also shrink from the reductionism of a non-realist notion of God – the idea that God is nothing more than a product of human imagination.

Thankfully, we are not faced with an either/or choice between these two positions. A third option, or rather, a range of options exists, clustered around a central position known as *critical realism*. A critical realist understanding of God-talk maintains that there is an objectively knowable reality called God who exists independently of human minds, but then stresses that this reality cannot be described in any literal sense; that all the models, metaphors and images we use to speak of God are mere human devices to grapple with that which is unspeakable.

literal realism	critical realism	non-realism

'But hang on a minute', I hear someone say, 'haven't we just jumped a stage? What exactly is the basis for religious realism – literal or critical?' The short answer to the question is that there is no independently verifiable basis for belief in religious realism. That doesn't mean that religious belief is illogical or absurd; plenty of very reasonable arguments exist to support religious faith, as some of the greatest minds in history have demonstrated. But none of this will add up to verifiable proof. That said, it can equally be argued that there is no verifiable proof that God does *not* exist. Both realist and non-realist positions are in fact based on presuppositions; both are essentially faith commitments.

Paul Ricoeur treats faith as a 'wager' – a bet, a venture, a gamble – based on the hunch that the claims of Christianity are not irrational or senseless, but worthwhile contemplating, worthwhile testing, worthwhile indwelling, worthwhile living out; that 'there is something of crucial importance to be interpreted in the fullness of biblical language.'[1]

For Ricoeur, faith is a matter of entering a hermeneutical circle – not a vicious circle, but a living and stimulating circle – which can be stated bluntly as: 'We must understand in order to believe, but we must believe in order to understand.'[2] In other words, it is impossible to pursue the journey of faith without daring to take a risk, without venturing a 'bet', without adopting the presupposition that the biblical texts are 'about something' rather than about nothing.[3]

Ricoeur's 'first naiveté' is a literal realism; it is about taking religious texts and dogma at face value. Once this original naiveté is shattered, there is no way back: something of the 'immediacy of belief' is irretrievably lost. But as we have already seen, Ricoeur envisages a 'second naiveté', which by definition falls into the territory of a critical realism – a way to 'believe again' without taking on board the baggage of literalism.[4]

A 'critical realist' faith takes it as given that God-talk is inescapably metaphorical, that God can be depicted through words, images and imaginative language, but never described or spoken of directly. Consequently, all God-talk is provisional, a point that C. S. Lewis expresses exquisitely in his 'Footnote to all Prayers':

He whom I bow to only knows to whom I bow
When I attempt the ineffable Name, murmuring Thou,
And dream of Pheidian fancies and embrace in heart
Symbols (I know) which cannot be the thing Thou art.
Thus always, taken at their word, all prayers blaspheme
Worshipping with frail images a folk-lore dream,
And all men in their praying, self-deceived, address
The coinage of their own unquiet thoughts, unless
Thou in magnetic mercy to Thyself divert
Our arrows, aimed unskillfully, beyond desert;

And all men are idolaters, crying unheard
To a deaf idol, if Thou take them at their word.

Take not, O Lord, our literal sense. Lord, in thy great
Unbroken speech our limping metaphor translate.[5]

A metaphor is a way of understanding one thing by likening it to something else. This presents the inevitable danger of
confusing the metaphorical image with the reality to which
it attempts to point. In religious terms, the result of this is
idolatry – we confuse something human with God. As a way
of countering this, Ricoeur insists that there is an 'is' and an 'is
not' contained in every metaphor.[6] So, for example, if we say
'God is Mother', we are not defining God as mother, or assert-
ing an identity between the terms 'God' and 'mother', which
would be idolatrous. Rather, we are attempting to consider
something that we do not know how to talk about – relating
to God – by likening it to something that we can talk about
– motherhood.[7]

In speaking of God, a delicate balance must be maintained
between idolatry and irrelevance.[8] God-talk becomes idolatrous when we forget the distance between our words and the
divine reality. However, it becomes irrelevant and meaningless
when it fails to resonate in ways that foster a profound connectedness with the divine. The two issues come together in
the image of God as father, which for some has become abso-
lutized and therefore idolatrous, and for others excluding and
therefore irrelevant.

The concern to retain this balance in God-talk is far from
new. Throughout history theologians and church leaders have
been eager to maintain the necessary distance between the unspeakable reality or essence of God, and the words and images
we use to speak of God and to address God. This distance
has been preserved in the Eastern branches of the Church by
distinguishing between *apophaticism* and *cataphaticism*, two
quite different approaches to theology.

Apophatic theology (otherwise known as negative theology,

or *via negativa*) stresses that God-talk is used against a background of human ignorance of the nature of God. But this ignorance is not so much a naive ignorance as a kind of acquired ignorance, an 'unknowing'. Apophatic theology is the recognition that, despite the huge amount of things we do say about God, there is really very little we can say about God. In a radical way, apophatic theology acknowledges divine transcendence, the absolute 'otherness' of God. The irony in the term 'apophatic theology' is that 'theology' means 'discourse about God', whereas 'apophatic' in effect means 'nothing to say about God'. So 'apophatic theology' ought to mean something like: 'that speech about God which is the failure of speech'.[9] Apophatic theology, or the *via negativa*, represents the purging of idolatrous God-talk. It directs us away from any glib assumption that we understand God or can speak of God directly. It is the path of silence before the divine.

By contrast, cataphatic theology, or the *via positiva*, is highly talkative. In his highly illuminating book, *The Darkness of God*, Denys Turner, the philosopher and theologian, describes cataphatic theology as: 'The Christian mind deploying all the resources of language in the effort to express something about God, and in that straining to speak, theology uses as many voices as it can.' It is the cataphatic element in God-talk that causes its 'metaphor-ridden' character to borrow vocabularies by analogy from everywhere and anywhere: 'Whether of science, literature, art, sex, politics, the law, the economy, family life, warfare, play, teaching, physiology, or whatever.' Cataphatic God-talk is 'a kind of verbal riot, an anarchy of discourse in which anything goes'.[10]

The tension between apophatic and cataphatic approaches to God-talk is crucial in preserving us from idolatry on the one hand, and irrelevance on the other. The cataphatic element incites us to 'name' God in a thousand different ways; the apophatic element reminds us that all our namings of God are provisional, tentative and revisable.

But who is this God we seek, both in the silence of unknowing, and in the 'verbal riot' of our God-talk? The spiritual quest is not about trying to encompass God, or encapsulate him in some theological formula. It is more about understanding the character of God. Marcus Borg, the liberal religious writer, suggests that there are two primary ways in which people understand God's character.[11] Whether the two are complete contrasts or whether they might combine in some way, he leaves it to the reader to decide. Both are certainly contained in the Bible and within Christian tradition. Nevertheless, the two approaches can lead to entirely different outcomes in terms of the way we live out and express our Christian faith.

In the first way of imagining God's character, God is a God of *requirements and rewards*. Borg links this approach to 'the monarchical model of God', which tends to formulate our relationship to God in legal terms. 'We have been disobedient to God's laws and deserve punishment, but God has provided a way of dealing with sin through sacrifice and repentance, with the death of Jesus understood as the sacrifice that makes forgiveness and salvation possible.'[12] If we believe this we can be saved and rewarded.

In its more extreme form, Borg points out, this is the God of the *Left Behind* novels, the God who will rescue and save some people at the second coming, but condemn vast swathes of humankind to eternal death and torment. But in a less extreme form, the 'requirements and rewards' understanding of God finds expression in a widespread belief that Christian living is all about meeting certain requirements. It focuses on a relationship with God based on obedience.

The second way that Borg identifies for imagining God's character sees God as a *God of love and justice*. This is certainly a very common theme in scripture. 'The prophets of the Hebrew Bible use the language of love to speak of God's relation to Israel. God is the lover, Israel the beloved.' The book of Hosea is a particularly good example of this, where God says, 'I will allure her, and bring her into the wilderness, and speak tenderly to her ... There she shall respond to me as in the days of her youth.'[13]

The God of love is also the God of justice. The two themes

are deeply interconnected. As Borg says, in the Bible justice is the social form of love. So the God of love is not simply some pink and fluffy deity, but one with a passion for justice. 'God loves everybody and everything, including the nonhuman world – not just me, and not just me and you, and not just us.'[14] I find it very reassuring to understand God as the one who loves with such zeal that justice must be sought and achieved. This is surely a theme that resonates deeply in our own world, where growing numbers of people believe that poverty must be made history, that the earth must be loved and treated with respect.

The outcome of a 'God of love and justice' understanding of God is bound to be quite different from an understanding based on a God of 'requirements and rewards'. 'The Christian life is about a relationship with God that transforms us into more compassionate beings. The God of love and justice is the God of relationship and transformation.' As Borg comments, 'What's at stake in the question of God's character is our image of the Christian life. Is Christianity about requirements? Here's what you must do to be saved. Or is Christianity about relationship and transformation? Here's the path: follow it. Both involve imperatives, but one is a threat, the other an invitation.'[15]

The understanding of God that drove Rosie away from home, away from church and from Christianity, sat firmly in the 'requirements and rewards' category. She experienced God as a heartless lawgiver, who required so much but gave so little. The only reward she truly wanted was to be loved and accepted for who she was. In the absence of that love, she went in search of it elsewhere.

In the course of Andrew's presentation in our dialogue with Philoso-Forum, he too spoke of an experience of Christianity that drove him out of the Church. When he was around twelve years old, he was riding his bike in the local woods during the summer holidays. It was a glorious day, so he stopped and stood still in a glade, where he felt an ecstatic oneness with the birds, the flowers, the trees and the sunshine. He had never experienced anything like it before. With excitement, he related the whole thing to his Sunday school teacher. But when the teacher heard Andrew's talk of 'the spirits of the trees, the flowers and the birds', a frown came over his face. It sounded too much like paganism to him. So he scolded Andrew, telling him that birds and trees do not have spirits. Reflecting on the experience, Andrew said that, had his teacher interpreted this experience in the light of divine immanence – God's presence within creation – he probably would have been a Christian rather than a Pagan.

The quest for God takes place at various levels in the human being, yet we so often address the matter solely at the rational or intellectual level. As Richard Holloway, writer and broadcaster, comments, 'This is why arguments about religion are usually inconclusive and unsatisfying and can sometimes be demoralizing for the intelligent believer' – and I would like to add, for the honest, open-hearted person who doesn't yet know how to believe. Faith in God does have an inescapably rational side to it, but faith is about something more: it is about responding to the mystery of the universe that is broader and more comprehensive than the mind alone can comprehend.

C. S. Lewis wrote:

As to why God does not make his existence demonstrably clear: are we sure that he is even interested in the kind of Theism that would be a compelled logical assent to a conclusive argument? Are we interested in it in personal matters? I demand from my friends a trust in my good faith which is certain without demonstrative proof. It wouldn't be confidence at all if he waited for rigorous proof. The magnanimity, the generosity which will trust on a reasonable probability is required of us. But supposing one believed and was wrong after all? Why, then, you would have paid the universe a compliment it doesn't deserve. Your error would even so be more interesting and important than the reality. And yet how could that be? How could an idiotic universe have produced creatures whose mere dreams are so much stronger, better, subtler than itself?[16]

Notes

1 Mark I. Wallace, *The Second Naiveté: Barth, Ricoeur, and the New Yale Theology*, Macon, Georgia: Mercer University Press, 1995, p. 27.

2 Paul Ricoeur, *The Symbolism of Evil*, Boston: Beacon Press, 1967, p. 351.

3 Wallace, *The Second Naiveté*, p. 112.

4 Ricoeur, *Symbolism*, p. 351f.

5 C. S. Lewis, *Poems*, London: Geoffrey Bles, 1964, p. 129.

6 Paul Ricoeur, *The Rule of Metaphor*, London: Routledge, 1978, p. 248f.

7 Sallie McFague, *Models of God: Theology for an Ecological, Nuclear Age*, London: SCM Press, 1987, p. 34.

8 Sallie McFague, *Metaphorical Theology: Models of God in Religious Language*, London: SCM Press, 1982, p. 145.

9 Denys Turner, *The Darkness of God: Negativity in Christian Mysticism*, Cambridge: Cambridge University Press, 1995, p. 19f.

10 Turner, *The Darkness*, p. 20.

11 Marcus Borg, *The Heart of Christianity: How We Can Be Passionate Believers Today*, New York: HarperCollins, 2003, p. 75ff.

12 Borg, *The Heart*, p. 75.

13 Borg, *The Heart*, p. 75.

14 Borg, *The Heart*, p. 76.

15 Borg, *The Heart*, p. 77f.

16 C. S. Lewis and S. Kilby, *A Mind Awake: An Anthology of C. S. Lewis*, New York: Harcourt Brace, 2003, p. 22.

6

Who is Christ for Us Today?

A question that never stands still

In a conversation with Gandhi in which the Mahatma had extolled the virtues of Jesus, the missionary E. Stanley Jones asked if he had ever considered becoming a Christian. 'I love your Christ,' Gandhi replied, 'I do not like your Christians. They are so unlike your Christ.' Apparently, Gandhi's rejection of Christianity stemmed from an incident when he was practising law in South Africa. He had been attracted to Christianity and studied the Bible and found the teachings of Jesus particularly appealing. But when he tried to attend a church service he was barred entry and told: 'There's no room for kaffirs in this church.' Gandhi left the church sorrowful, and determined never again to consider becoming a Christian.

No doubt the church that turned Gandhi away considered themselves 'orthodox'. I'm sure their christology (their doctrine of the nature of Jesus Christ) was perfectly orthodox. But to Gandhi, all that mattered was the fact that their doctrine of Jesus Christ did not stop them from turning him away. Like so many Christians, they failed to grasp that practice is the touchstone against which a christology's authenticity has to be tested. We believe in God by the way we live, not just by the way we formulate our theology. As Jürgen Moltmann argues, 'Every christology is related to christopraxis: what we know and what we do belong together.'[1] A re-enchanted Christianity is a lived Christianity.

Gandhi's experience demonstrates that believing in Jesus is a political affair. It always is. And our political presuppositions will influence the way we believe in Jesus and the way we interpret scripture, as the situation in South Africa under apartheid demonstrated, where thoroughly 'Bible-believing' Christians used scripture to justify structural racism and discrimination.

Marcus Borg makes the point that Christians in the United States are deeply divided about what it means to follow Jesus – basically, because they do not share the same socio-political outlook:

- Many followers of Jesus oppose evolution and defend the literal-factual truth of the Bible's stories of creation. Yet followers of Jesus were the first to reconcile evolution with the Bible by understanding the Genesis stories symbolically and not literally.
- Followers of Jesus are among the strongest supporters of our nation's invasion and continuing occupation of Iraq. Followers of Jesus are among its strongest critics.
- Followers of Jesus are among the strongest opponents of gay marriage. Followers of Jesus are among its strongest advocates.
- Followers of Jesus are among the strongest supporters of an economic and tax policy that benefits especially the wealthy and powerful. Followers of Jesus are among its most vocal critics on the biblical grounds that such policy betrays God's passion for economic justice for the poor.

Examples could be multiplied, but these are sufficient to illustrate the sharp disagreement among Christians about what it means to take Jesus seriously. 'Our culture wars are to a considerable extent Jesus wars', Borg writes.[2]

One of the most important questions to be asked in the search for re-enchanted Christianity is the one posed by Dietrich Bonhoeffer, the theologian executed by the Nazis, when he wrote: 'What is bothering me incessantly is the question what Christianity really is, or indeed who Christ really is, for us today.'[3] Clearly, this was a question with profound political ramifications for Bonhoeffer: he was imprisoned and ultimately executed by the Nazis for plotting to assassinate Hitler. Rightly or wrongly, he believed that such an act was required by his faith in Christ.

The question, 'Who is Christ for us today?' can never go away. Every new generation of Christians must grapple with it afresh. Speaking personally, it is not a question that embroils me in the metaphysical disputes and conundrums of Nicea or Chalcedon. For, important and fascinating as the disputes and arguments surrounding the ecumenical councils are, they represent the problems of another age, of another set of seekers trying to comprehend who Jesus really is – human or divine or both – and what is the significance of his life and death and resurrection. The answers forged in the fourth or fifth centuries have little interest to most people in the twenty-first century.

'Who is Christ for us today?' The question can never stand still, because the context in which it is asked does not stand still. The significance of the figure of Jesus Christ, of his life, his teaching and his actions, requires constant reinterpretation in order for it to continue to bring hope, liberation and wisdom to a changing world. Today, this means asking who is Christ for women as well as men, for the poor world as well as the rich, for gay people as well as straight, for immigrants and asylum seekers, for techies, jet-setters, environmentalists, poets, artists and twenty-first-century misfits. Who is Jesus Christ in our tense and complex, multicultural, multi-faith global village, bursting with beauty, terror and opportunity?

One thing that remains constant for Christians trying to work out who Christ really is for us today is the affirmation that Jesus is the decisive revelation of God: Jesus discloses what God looks like in a human life, and what a life filled with God looks like. For Christians, divine revelation is not finally in a text, a creed or a set of dogmas, but in a person; not in words, but in a living Word. 'As Son of God, Christ reveals God; as the Word made flesh, he embodies what can be seen of God in a human life; as the Light of the World, he enlightens us about the nature and will of God and about the way to life.'[4]

Yet importantly, as Marcus Borg points out, Jesus is not the revelation of 'all' of God, but of what can be seen of God in a human life:

> Some of God's traditional attributes or qualities cannot be seen in a human life. The omnipresence of God cannot be seen in a human life – a human being cannot be present everywhere. The infinity of God cannot be seen in a human life – a human being by definition is finite. So also omniscience: what could it mean to say that a human is 'omniscient' and that Jesus in particular was? That he would 'know everything' – including, for example, the theory of relativity and the capital of Oregon?[5]

This isn't going to sit well with lots of Christians, many of whom inadvertently stray very close to the early heresy of Docetism – a doctrine that stresses the divinity of Christ to the exclusion of his humanity. In their zeal to acclaim and defend Christ's divinity, many modern Christians edge very close to Docetism, virtually denying Christ's humanity with a mistaken supernaturalism. Jesus did not know everything – of course he didn't! Jesus made judgements that were less than perfect – of course he did! Jesus believed things about the world and the universe that we now know to be untrue – of course he did! He was a first-century man. Jesus picked his nose, broke wind, and got impatient with his friends – of course he did, because these are the kind of things involved in being human. Nevertheless, in a decisive way – in and through his humanity – the character of God was manifested in Jesus of Nazareth. And this is what the incarnation proclaims: God inhabiting human life, without in any way violating or abrogating human nature.

How did the incarnation work? How was 'the Word made flesh'? Frankly, I don't know. And the technicalities don't bother me much. The incarnation is the central mystery within the Christian tradition. However, I see no reason why faith in the incarnation necessarily hinges on, or is intrinsically bound up with, belief in a miraculous conception and birth. I respect the views of people who do believe it to be true, but I agree with the overwhelming consensus of mainstream scholarly opinion that the birth narratives are metaphorical rather than historical.

It may seem like a fudge to say that the stories of Christ's birth are metaphorical. But it really isn't. And it's certainly not a way of debunking them or the truth they convey. Only the doggedly rationalist mind imagines that truth is equated solely with fact.

From a scholarly perspective, one key reason for treating the birth narratives as metaphorical rather than factual is that they are relatively late developments in the early Christian tradition, found only in Matthew's and Luke's Gospels, which were written eighty or more years after Christ's birth. No mention of a special birth is made in either Mark, the earliest Gospel, or in the writings of Paul, which are the most primitive in the New Testament. And John makes no reference to it, either – at least, not in any direct narrative form. If stories of Jesus' miraculous birth were important and early in Christian tradition, it is hard to imagine why they are absent in Mark, Paul, John and the rest of the New Testament.[6]

Paul's main reference to Christ's birth is this: 'When the fullness of time had come, God sent forth his Son, born of a woman, born under the law' (Gal. 4.4). As John Macquarrie, theologian and philosopher, comments, this is a verse that sets Jesus 'fully and firmly within the human race': like every other human being, Jesus was 'born of a woman'; and also, like every other human being, he was born into a specific culture, 'born under the law', the most important feature of the Jewish people. There is nothing here to suggest that Jesus was conceived or born in any special way; he was thoroughly human. Yet this did not hinder Paul from affirming that he is 'Son of God'.[7]

The stories of Jesus' birth are not primarily concerned with a biological miracle, but with the assertion that God was present in Christ in a decisive way; that he was not simply the product of natural evolution nor even of human procreation, but that there is something 'more' in Jesus. There is also a strong intention in Matthew's Gospel to connect Christ's birth with Isaiah's prophecy (Isa. 7.14) that a young woman ('virgin' is a mistranslation) would conceive and bear a son who would be called Immanuel – God with us.[8]

The early Church believed that God had entered human experience in a decisive fashion in the person of Jesus Christ, and a tradition emerged that expressed that belief in the glorious stories of his conception and birth narrated by Matthew and Luke, which have fired the imagination of millions throughout history, particularly in the celebration of Christmas. The central point of Christian faith and theology is this: that 'God was in Christ'. It is no more necessary for me to believe that this came about through a virgin birth than it is to think that the only way God could create the world is according to the narratives in Genesis 1 and 2.

The really important point for most Christians to grapple with concerning Christ's incarnation is *who Jesus Christ really is for us today.*

The Benedictine sister, Joan Chittister, states that when she utters the words of the Apostle's Creed, 'I believe in Jesus', she is saying:

> I believe in a way of life above and beyond what anything else challenges me to be. Institutions, the best of them, want me in the end for the aggrandizement, the status, the power, the service of themselves. They want me to keep their rules and regulations, their laws and disciplines, their priorities and prescriptions, all of them, without a doubt, good. But all of them partial. Short of the goal. Only Jesus wants me for more than that. Jesus wants me for the gospel, for the Good Life, whatever the cost. That is the Jesus in whom I believe.[9]

The important issue raised by the question of who Christ really is for us today is not primarily about which boxes of 'orthodoxy' we will tick, but rather, how will we live out the liberating, life-affirming, peace-making, people-redeeming good news of Christ in the world today. This links right into the other half of Bonhoeffer's question: 'What is bothering me incessantly is the question what Christianity really is.' What does it mean to believe in Christ and follow Christ today?

Virtually every New Testament scholar agrees that the central concern and passion of Jesus is the kingdom of God. It is impossible to follow Christ or to understand who he is today without getting involved with God's kingdom. What does that mean?

The kingdom of God is basically God's programme to transform the world, both on a personal and a societal level. 'The kingdom of God is what the world would be if God were directly and immediately in charge.'[10] The problem with the word 'kingdom' is that to our ears today it tends to denote privilege, exclusion and hierarchy. Whereas the layers of meaning in the original Aramaic and Greek words, *malkuta* and *basileia* – both of which are feminine words – suggest something more egalitarian and liberating, a quality of leadership that enables and *empowers* rather than dominates. *Malkuta* also means 'counsel' or 'advice', so God's kingdom is that state of things in which God's guidance is carried out, resulting in a state of empowerment. To pray 'Your kingdom come' is to ask that our personal and collective attitudes be aligned with God's good counsels.

Conservative Christians tend to major on the personal aspects of proclaiming God's kingdom – the call to be born again, and the like – whereas more liberal or progressive Christians emphasize the kingdom message in terms of transforming society. For Jesus, there was no distinction between the two: the message of the kingdom is directed at both personal and social transformation.

John Dominic Crossan, the Irish–American religious scholar, suggests that we replace the term 'kingdom of God' with 'a companionship of empowerment'.[11] This certainly echoes the sense of the Aramaic word *malkuta*, which Jesus himself would have used. I personally think of the kingdom of God as *a universal culture of life, hope and liberation.* Proclaiming God's kingdom means bringing healing to broken lives, healing to a broken world.

Whether the focus is on the personal or collective aspects, proclaiming God's kingdom is a political activity. When Jesus brought liberation and hope to the poor and the oppressed, he empowered them to rise up and resist tyranny and injustice in God's name. And this is why the authorities executed Jesus – not because he was a healer, or a mystic, or a wisdom teacher, but because he liberated people in such a way and on such a scale that they presented a perceived threat to the powers. A christological spirituality is a kingdom of God spirituality, which is also a politically engaged spirituality.

Archbishop Desmond Tutu contested the tyranny of apartheid in South Africa, not because he is a politician but because he is a Christian asking who Christ really is for us today. In his Charge to the Provincial Synod in 1992, where the motion was passed to ordain women priests, he said:

We are a church on the move, an instrument in the hand of God, proclaiming the Good News, nurturing new converts, we are instruments of peace and reconciliation and justice in the hands of God. We are the means of healing hurts, of building community, of feeding the hungry. We are a worshipping Spirit-filled community, who know that we can do God's work only in God's way with God's means, and so we have an engaged spirituality that places first things first.

We are God's partners, God's agents of transfiguration, to change the ugliness of the world, its hatred, its hostilities, its jealousies, its hunger, its poverty, its injustice, its oppression, its alienation, its loneliness, its rivalry, its competitiveness, its grasping, its sickness, into their glorious counterparts; so that there will be laughter and joy, caring and sharing, justice, reconciliation and peace, compassion.

Tutu's determination to proclaim the kingdom of God, to spread a universal culture of life, hope and liberation made him a threat to the political powers in South Africa. He and his family received constant death threats from apartheid supporters. But he continued with his campaign because he was gripped by the question of who Christ really is for us today.

I find the courage of Desmond Tutu deeply inspiring. I also find the courage of Gandhi, who wasn't a Christian, highly inspirational. Both men manifest the heart and character of God. It would be absurd to suggest otherwise. Is such a view at odds with the Christian affirmation that God is revealed decisively in Jesus Christ? Only if we claim that genuine knowledge of God is found in Jesus Christ *and in him alone*. I don't believe that. I shall enlarge on this point later in the book; for now, sufficient to say that I reject both the exclusivist approach to Christianity (there is no truth or genuine relation to God outside of the Christian faith), and the relativist approach (all beliefs are equally valid). Instead, I take an approach of 'openness and commitment'[12] – I make no bones about my own faith commitment, but I remain constantly open to encountering God in other ways.

From my childhood I have loved Jesus Christ. My theological and spiritual framework for expressing who I see him to be has changed vastly over the years, but my love for him and my commitment to what he is about has only deepened with time. Yet still I find myself 'bothered incessantly' by the question of who Christ really is for us today.

Notes

1 Jürgen Moltmann, *Jesus Christ for Today's World*, London: SCM Press, 1994, p. 2.

2 Marcus Borg, *Jesus: Uncovering the Life, Teachings, and Relevance of a Religious Revolutionary*, New York: HarperCollins, 2006, p. 4f.

3 Dietrich Bonhoeffer, *Letters and Papers from Prison*, London: SCM Press, 1971, p. 279.

4 Borg, *Jesus*, p. 6f.

5 Borg, *Jesus*, p. 6f.

6 Borg, *Jesus*, p. 61.

7 John Macquarrie, *Christology Revisited*, London: SCM Press, 1998, p. 31.

8 John Macquarrie, *Christology Revisited*, pp. 31–6.

9 Joan Chittister, *In Search of Belief*, Hampshire: Redemptorist Publications, 1999, p. 68.

10 John Dominic Crossan, *Jesus: A Revolutionary Biography*, New York: HarperCollins, 1994, p. 55.

11 John Dominic Crossan, in Marcus Borg (ed.), *Jesus at 2000*, New York: Basic Books, 1998, pp. 22–55.

12 The expression 'openness and commitment' has been especially raised by John Macquarrie in *Theology, Church and Ministry*, London: SCM Press, 1986, pp. 141–54, and John Cobb, *Liberal Christianity at the Crossroads*, Philadelphia: Westminster Press, 1973, p. 14.

7

Passion Stories

Trying to make sense of atonement

It is remarkable that the central iconic image of Christianity should be a symbol of execution – the Roman equivalent of an electric chair, a gas chamber or a firing squad. Of course, no one sat down and decided that the logo of the Church would be the cross – though any PR company would be very proud to have come up with the idea! It is straightforwardly the result of the execution of Jesus becoming the most important event in Christian history; indeed, in the history of Western civilization.

Jesus was killed because he was deemed an agitator: someone who spoke out against injustice, who denounced the religious authorities, who campaigned dramatically against temple corruption, and, worst of all, who was highly popular with the masses. Jesus was a Jewish mystic, a healer, an exorcist and a charismatic teacher. But he wasn't killed for any of these: he was killed for upending the *status quo* – for eating with the wrong people, for ridiculing the pomposity of religious leaders by stating that they would trail behind prostitutes and tax collectors in entering the kingdom of heaven, for preaching justice for the poor, for breaking ritualistic taboos, for treating women, children and Gentiles as persons in their own right, for placing the needs of people above fussy legalistic interpretations of the law. Jesus empowered those on the periphery of society – always a dangerous thing to do!

Yet Christians claim that there is more to it than this: that Jesus' death was not simply at the whim of the authorities but was part of a bigger plan by God to save the world. The theme is etched into our consciousness through countless films, songs, books and sermons – Jesus died to cleanse us from our sins, to obtain forgiveness for us, to reconcile us to God, and to ensure us a place in heaven. But the question many of us can't get out of our heads is 'why?' Why did Jesus have to die so that we could be forgiven? How does it work? Why would his death on the cross make a difference?

The Church encapsulates its answer to such questions in the doctrine of the atonement. To atone means to recompense a wrongdoing, to make reconciliation or to make amends for an injury. The doctrine of the atonement has been expressed through the ages in various forms, but the version of it that most of us are familiar with is commonly known as 'substitutionary atonement' or 'penal substitution'. According to this, Christ became our substitute on the cross, bearing our sins and the punishment we deserved. So, by trusting in the redeeming work of Christ, the wrath of God is averted, we find cleansing and forgiveness, and are made acceptable to God.

The moral and practical difficulties with this scenario are endless. It describes 'a transaction wholly within God's self'. But, as Walter Wink, specialist in biblical interpretation, asks, what is wrong with this God 'whose legal ledgers can be balanced only by means of the death of an innocent victim?'[1] Why is a sacrificial victim necessary to make forgiveness possible? How are we to make sense of a schizophrenic deity who all of a sudden changes his attitude towards people when another person dies in their place? Little wonder that many people turn their back on such a monstrous notion of God. As Wink says, 'Against such an image of God the revolt of atheism is an act of pure religion!'[2]

Yet tragically, this is the image of God that is routinely preached and taught in most churches. It is hard to imagine that those who preach it have ever truly contemplated what it is they are saying. But the reality that is seldom acknowledged is that this doctrine of substitutionary atonement is just one of a number of theological models or interpretations of the significance of Christ's death. We will look at some others later, but first let me suggest that there are four important windows through which to observe the Good Friday events and make sense their significance.

WINDOWS ON ATONEMENT

historical facts	metaphysical significance
theological interpretation	personal & collective impact

The *first window* looks at the historical facts surrounding the death of Christ. We do not have a great deal of verifiable information, but we do know that Jesus of Nazareth was a real man; that he was a popular healer and wisdom teacher, and that the Romans, in collusion with the Jewish temple authorities, executed him. But, of course, he was one of thousands who died at the hands of the Romans. The fact that he existed and died indicates nothing about the religious significance of his death.

For that, we must look to the *second window*, which can be viewed only with the eye of faith. Christians claim that Christ's death had metaphysical or spiritual consequences. Something happened in the spiritual realm as a result. The crucifixion changed things in some significant way.

The *third window* is in fact a number of windows – the theological interpretations that are given to the historical facts and their perceived metaphysical significance. Since no one can get behind the events of Good Friday and see precisely what they achieved in the heavenly realm, we need imaginative models that can help us understand and interpret the significance of Christ's death. But we should never forget that is what they are: models and metaphors that are open to question and revision.

Lastly, there is the *fourth window* of human experience. Throughout history people and whole communities have testified to the impact that the death of Christ has had on their lives. It has shaped history, brought hope and liberation to millions, and injected meaning into incalculable suffering and misery. The death of Christ – or more precisely, the whole Christ event – has indeed transformed people's lives.

To recognize these four windows on Christ's Passion, and to distinguish between them, can be very liberating – not least, in confirming that the substitutionary interpretation is just that: an interpretation, one that many people reject as being unhelpful, illogical and inconsistent with their notion and vision of who and what God is like. I am one of those people.

Theological models of the atonement fall into three main categories. The oldest of these, which held sway for a thousand years, is known as *Christus Victor*, or the *Ransom* model. According to this, the devil held captive the souls of humankind because of their sin. Through some sort of contractual agreement, God handed his Son over to the devil in exchange for humankind's release. The devil then killed Jesus, but in a surprise turn of events Jesus rose from the dead and triumphed over the hoards of darkness. This is basically the model that C. S. Lewis depicts in *The Lion, the Witch and the Wardrobe*, where Aslan, the great lion, allows himself to be killed by the wicked witch so that Edmund can be freed from her icy grip. After this, Aslan returns alive and well to conquer her forces.

Anselm of Canterbury introduced the *satisfaction* or *substitutionary* model of atonement in the eleventh century. He believed that Christ's death was necessary to satisfy the offended honour of God, and thereby restore divine order to the universe. The background to this theory is the medieval world of feudal hierarchy in which Anselm lived. The Catholic theologian Richard McBrien, who argues that Anselm's theory seems to distort rather than illuminate the meaning of Christ's mission, writes:

Anselm's theory is to be understood against the background of the Germanic and early medieval feudal system. There is a bond of honour between the feudal lord and vassal. Infringement of the lord's honour is tantamount to an assault upon the whole feudal system. A demand for satisfaction, therefore, is not for the sake of appeasing the lord's personal sense of honour but for the sake of restoring order to the 'universe' (feudal system) in which, and therefore against which, the 'sin' was committed. The feudal lord cannot simply overlook the offense, because the order of his whole economic and social world is at stake. So too with God.[3]

The Protestant Reformers modified Anselm's interpretation, giving it a more explicitly legal framework. Human sin is an offence against divine law, which must be punished. By accepting that punishment on behalf of humankind, Jesus substitutes his righteousness for our sin, which is why this model is sometimes called 'penal substitution'.

The third atonement model, articulated by Peter Abelard, also in the eleventh century, is known as *moral influence*. Abelard rejects the notion of a debt needing to be paid for sin. The problem to be solved in his view is the estrangement between humans and God. The incarnation and death of Christ bring about reconciliation through example: Christ's life, his willingness to absorb hatred by forgiving his killers from the cross, and his resurrection life all convey to humanity God's transforming love. So, according to Abelard it is through the heartbreaking realization of God's unstoppable love for humanity that we are transformed and freed from the power of sin and selfishness.

I find that a combination of Abelard's model of atonement together with a revised version of *Christus Victor* helps me to make sense of the cross and its significance in God's redemptive purposes. But before I say more about that, let me make a few other general comments.

First, I do not believe that Jesus died in order that God would forgive our sins. Jesus forgave people's sins constantly in the Gospels, long before he died on the cross, and he taught his disciples to pray for forgiveness with every expectation that it would be granted. God always forgives. It is in God's nature to forgive. God's forgiveness is unilateral – we are forgiven whether or not we choose to accept that forgiveness. The God of Jesus Christ is characterized by grace and love, not wrath, anger or retribution.

The parable of the Prodigal Son offers a radical critique of the angry God presented in substitutionary atonement. Clearly the father had forgiven the son before he even left for the far-off land – forgiveness is not an issue in this story. The son's redemption hinged on his remembrance of his father's grace – 'How many of my Father's hired hands have bread enough and to spare?' When the son returned, no retribution was required, no threat of punishment hung over his head. The father absorbed the pain and stupidity of his son's waywardness and welcomed him back unreservedly, just as he forgave his older son's self-righteousness and judgementalism. Forgiveness was always in the father's heart; the only question was whether his son would receive it and live in the good of it.

Jesus proclaimed the unconditional love and acceptance of God throughout his ministry. He spread a culture of life, hope and liberation; he made the loving, healing, challenging reign of God a visible reality in the world, and he delivered people from the 'demons' of prejudice, mental and emotional abuse, self-loathing, social injustice and false images of God. Jesus empowered the most disadvantaged people in society, and he removed the temple authorities' institutionalized monopoly on forgiveness – which was an instrument of social control and financial gain. His mission was profoundly subversive, and threatened the religious authorities so much that they conspired to kill him. God did not require Jesus' death in order to grant forgiveness, and Jesus did not will himself to die, though he was willing to die in order to demonstrate the unending love and forgiveness of God in the face of hatred and mindless scapegoating.

The substitutionary theory reflects an image of God that I

cannot accept. Looking at it from the perspective of domestic abuse, pastor Thelma Megill-Cobbler notes that even the softer notion of substitutionary atonement, in which God *allows* rather than desires or inflicts 'the punishment of the child', fits the pattern of abusive family systems (as when a parent passively observes his or her spouse beating their child). God thus becomes the model abuser.

> At their most extreme, penal theories threaten to divide the Trinity, depicting the Father as a vindictive judge, and the Son as the loving saviour who is willing that humanity be saved, meekly enduring an undeserved death. Perhaps the Son is for us, but the Father appears to be against both us and the Son.[4]

Peter Abelard, Anselm's younger contemporary, protested, 'Indeed, how cruel and wicked it seems that anyone should demand the blood of an innocent person as the price for anything, or that it should in any way please him that an innocent man should be slain – still less that God should consider the death of his Son so agreeable that by it he should be reconciled to the whole world!' As Walter Wink says, the problem is that substitutionary theory portrays God as a cruel and unforgiving patriarch 'unable to love as a decent parent should, trapped in his own rules that force him to commit a ghastly crime. In that view it is God who needs forgiveness, not us!'[5] Substitutionary atonement theory could be seen as 'a crime against divinity!'

Each of the atonement models has some basis in scripture, yet the Bible offers no systematized atonement theory. It is often assumed that substitutionary atonement is strongly supported in the epistle to the Hebrews, which represents a thorough-going reinterpretation of Israel's ancient sacrificial culture. However, the idea that Hebrews expounds substitutionary theory is strongly contested. The trick is to find a way to read Hebrews without looking through the lens of substitutionary atonement theory – which was, of course, formulated a thousand years after Hebrews was written. There can be no doubting that sacrifice and the language of sacrifice are intrinsic to the rhetoric of the epistle. 'But how that rhetoric was designed and which elements of the discourse of sacrifice are assumed, tolerated, modified, or embraced is another question.'[6]

Some commentators argue that Hebrews actually overturns substitutionary theory rather than supports it; that the epistle subverts sacrificial language under the cover of sacrificial language. It is beyond my present scope to expand much on the argument; sufficient to say that it turns on the use of Psalm 40 in Hebrews 10.5–8. This appears in the midst of the writer's critique of the law, which he says is a mere shadow of the good things to come. The words of the psalm are then placed on the lips of the pre-incarnate Christ:

Sacrifices and offerings you have not desired,
   but a body you have prepared for me;
in burnt offerings and sin-offerings
   you have taken no pleasure.

The sacrificial system is definitively named and identified: sacrifices, burnt offerings and sin offerings. 'The citation of Psalm 40 makes clear that God does not desire sacrifices, nor were they something that he had ever wanted. In the editorial comment the author also adds that God was not pleased with them.' Instead, it is in taking on human flesh and in his doing the will of God that Jesus becomes the author of salvation.[7]

René Girard, historian, literary critic and philosopher, argues that Jesus' death revealed the sacrificial system as a form of organized violence in the service of social tranquillity. The sacrificial system is like a vaccination, in which a smaller amount of violence is perpetrated against a single victim in order to prevent a greater amount of evil from engulfing society. Caiaphas articulated the scapegoat mechanism when he said that it was better for Jesus to die than for the nation to be plunged into war (John 11.50).[8]

The cross is the point in history where the cries of the sac-

rificed and the scapegoated are vindicated. Jesus was not the
first or the last person to become a scapegoat. But by forgiving
his killers instead of voicing vengeance, he refused to succumb
to the perspective of the persecutors. Even in his reactions on
the cross, he rejected complicity in violence. Instead, through
his trial, crucifixion and death, Jesus 'stripped the scapegoating mechanism of its sacred aura and exposed it for what it
was: legalised murder'. Walter Wink adds that insofar as the
deaths of other witnesses (Oscar Romero, Martin Luther King,
Gandhi and others) reflect the same truth that was revealed in
his dying, 'they perpetuate its revelatory power'.[9] The outcome
of Girard's understanding of the death of Christ is that Jesus
was sent by God to be the *last* scapegoat and to reconcile us
once and for all to God, which is the basic message of the epistle to the Hebrews. So, Jesus became the sacrificial scapegoat,
not because God requires sacrificial scapegoats, but in order to
expose the scapegoating mechanism for what it is, and bring
it to an end.

As I have said, for me the significance of Christ's Passion is
best understood through aspects of Abelard's moral influence
model together with a contemporary reworking of *Christus
Victor* in which the cross is seen as God's victory of love and
justice over the powers of satan. The notion of sacrifice as
an act of unselfish love can be seen in both of these models
without resorting to the idea that God required a scapegoat in
order to grant forgiveness.

Walter Wink prefers to dub *Christus Victor* as 'the liberation theory of atonement', because that is what the term 'ransom' in Mark 10.45 means – 'For the son of man came not to
be served but to serve, and to give his life to *ransom/liberate*
many.' The *Christus Victor* or ransom model recognizes that
human beings require liberation from satan's power, and that
Christ opened up this possibility by confronting satan in and
through his death.

I largely accept Wink's reinterpretation of this model, including his view that 'satan' is not a personified entity but an
'archetypal reality'. 'If Satan is a reality at all', Wink says, 'it

is ... as a profound *experience* of numinous, uncanny power in the psychic and historic lives of real people. *Satan is the real interiority of a society that idolatrously pursues its own enhancement as the highest good.* Satan is the spirituality of an epoch, the peculiar constellation of alienation, greed, inhumanity, oppression, and entropy that characterizes a specific period of history as a consequence of human decisions to tolerate and even further such a state of affairs.'[10]

Wink argues that all manifestations of power in the world – the state, business corporations, economic structures, educational institutions and the like – have an inner and an outer aspect, a spiritual and a material dimension.[11] When a material structure is organized around things like greed, lies, enmity, prejudice, abuse, corruption or injustice, then it becomes a power or force opposed to the reign of God; it is driven by a 'demonic' spirituality.

Throughout his public ministry, Jesus posed a threat to the powers in his day, so they killed him. But their plan went awry. As they stripped him and humiliated him, they did not realize that the whole way of life that they defended was also being stripped and seen for what it was. As they nailed him to the cross, they failed to see that their systems of domination were being nailed and condemned.

In the injustice of the cross, Jesus took upon himself all the hatred, the scapegoating, the rebellion, the malice, the deceit, the prejudice and the abuse that were thrown at him, and still refused to respond in kind. He remained on course, 'on message' to the end. 'Forgive them, Father,' he cried, 'for they do not know what they are doing.'

Abelard's moral influence model is sometimes disparagingly referred to as a 'subjective' model, that is, it contains no element of change from God's side; it refers only to a change on the human side. Yet, whatever else it represents, the cross of Christ is a massively transforming revelation of divine love and grace. I prefer to think of the cross – and indeed, of the entire Christ-event – as the ultimate sacrament of divine love, the supreme means of God being present in the human condition in a way that is utterly transformational both personally and socially. The cross does not reconcile God to us; it reconciles us to God. Forgiveness was already given, but through his death Jesus performs and enacts God's forgiveness in the most resolute and vigorous fashion imaginable.

Jürgen Moltmann argues that the Passion of Christ is the Passion of God: that, in the death of Christ, God took death and pain and suffering into God's self. In contrast to the traditional idea of divine impassibility (the belief that God cannot experience pain or suffering), Moltmann contends that 'An almighty God who cannot suffer is poverty-stricken, because he cannot love.' The impact of a belief in the 'crucified God' on those who suffer can be transformational. 'People who believe in the God who suffers with us, recognize their suffering in God, and God in their suffering, and in companionship with him find the strength to remain in love and not to become bitter, in spite of pain and sorrow.'[12]

The cross is where we find the suffering God, entering into the pain of the world. Moltmann recalls being in Hamburg in July 1943, when he lay under the hail of bombs that rained down on his home town, annihilating 80,000 people in a storm of fire. In what seemed like a miracle, he lived through the attack. In that hell, he says, he did not ask: 'Why does God let this happen?' Rather, his question was: 'My God, where are you? Where is God? Is he far away from us, an absentee God in his own heaven? Or is he a sufferer among the sufferers? Does he share in our suffering? Do our sufferings cut him to the heart too?' The question: 'Why does God let this happen?' presupposes an apathetic God. By contrast, 'Where is God?' looks for a God who suffers with us.[13]

Christ's suffering is the passion of a passionate God. Moltmann makes reference to Catherine of Siena, who once cried out: 'My God and Lord, where were you when my heart was plunged in darkness and filth?' and she heard the answer: 'My daughter, did you not feel it? I was in your heart.'[14] In his book *Night*, Ellie Weisel tells of how he and other prisoners were forced to watch the hanging of a young boy in Auschwitz. As they silently watched the boy die a lingering death, a voice be-hind Weisel asked, 'Where is God now?' Weisel heard another voice within himself reply: 'Here he is – he is hanging here on this gallows.'[15]

The notion of Christ's suffering as the Passion of a passion-ate God is consonant with a synthesis of Abelard's model of moral influence and *Christus Victor*. In the cross we witness God's unwavering love bearing hatred and violence, and dis-empowering it at the same time. When received, such love transforms human lives and human society.

Love so amazing, so divine,
demands my soul, my life, my all.

The cross cannot be ignored or dismissed as a mere historical event. It is the *axis mundi*, the pivotal point in history, the epi-centre of divine love and grace, and the court of justice where all systems of domination and oppression are condemned.

Atonement has been defined by thousands of preachers as 'at-one-ment'. The cross is indeed the place where God invites us to be at one with God, with each other, and with ourselves. Madeleine L'Engle ponders that thought beautifully when she writes:

For Jesus, at-one-ment was not only being at-one with the glory of the stars, or the first daffodil in the spring, or a baby's laugh. He was also at-one with all the pain and suf-fering that ever was, is, or will be. On the cross Jesus was at-one with the young boy with cancer, the young mother haemorrhaging, the raped girl. And perhaps the most ter-rible anguish came from being at-one with the people of Sodom and Gomorrah, the death chambers at Belsen, the horrors of radiation in the destruction of Hiroshima and Nagasaki. It came from being at-one with the megalomania of the terrorist, the coldness of heart of 'good' people … We can withdraw, even in our prayers, from the intensity of suffering. Jesus, on the cross, experienced it all. When

I touch the small cross I wear, this, then, is the meaning of the symbol.[16]

Notes

1 Walter Wink, *The Powers That Be: Theology for a New Millennium*, New York: Doubleday, 1998, p. 87.

2 Wink, *The Powers*, p. 89.

3 Richard McBrien, *Catholicism Volume 1*, Minneapolis: Winston Press, 1980, p. 462.

4 Thelma Megill-Cobbler, 'A Feminist Rethinking of Punishment Imagery in Atonement', quoted in Walter Wink, *The Human Being: Jesus and the Enigma of the Son of Man*, Minneapolis: Fortress Press, 2002, p. 106.

5 Quoted in Wink, *The Human*, p. 106.

6 Loren L. Johns, 'A Better Sacrifice or Better than Sacrifice?', in William M. Swartley (ed.), *Violence Renounced: René Girard's Biblical Studies and Peacemaking*, Telford, Pennsylvania: Pandora Press US, 2000, p. 121.

7 Michael Hardin, 'Sacrificial Language in Hebrews: Reappraising René Girard', in Swartley, *Violence Renounced*, p. 112f .

8 My explanation of René Girard's views is taken mainly from Wink, *The Powers*, pp. 82–97. Further discussion of René Girard's non-violent interpretation of the atonement can be found in Swartley, *Violence Renounced*, and in J. Denny Weaver, *The Nonviolent Atonement*, Grand Rapids: Eerdmans, 2001.

9 Wink, *The Powers*, p. 86f.

10 Walter Wink, *Unmasking the Powers: The Invisible Forces That Determine Human Existence*, Philadelphia: Fortress Press, 1986, p. 24f.

11 Wink, *The Powers*, pp. 13–36.

12 Jürgen Moltmann, *Jesus Christ for Today's World*, London: SCM Press, 1994, p. 46.

13 Moltmann, *Jesus Christ*, p. 30f.

14 Moltmann, *Jesus Christ*, p. 46.

15 Ellie Weisel, *Night*, New York: Bantam Books, 1982, p. 61f.

16 Madeleine L'Engle, *Glimpses of Grace*, New York: HarperCollins, 1996, p. 77f.

8

Easter Surprise

What does Resurrection really mean?

The Easter Vigil is my favourite service of the entire year. It is a moment of re-enchantment, a piece of pure magic. This is how we keep the vigil at St Luke's.

At 11.15pm on the eve of Easter, the congregation are seated in a darkened church, lit only by seven large candles. The chairs are arranged in a circle, punctuated by six large candlesticks. In the centre is a small table on which stands the previous year's paschal candle (a tall candle that is renewed every Easter, which signifies Christ's presence in the church). The first half of the service consists of six Bible readings following the salvation story from the creation in Genesis to the death and burial of Jesus. After each reading, a candle is extinguished. Eventually, at about 11.45pm one final reading is given, from the Paschal Homily of St Chrysostom, after which the last candle is removed from the church, leaving the congregation sitting in complete darkness and silence for about ten minutes during which we feel the stillness of Christ's tomb.

On the stroke of midnight, as the church bell heralds the arrival of Easter Day, an intense flash sears the darkness (our own pyrotechnics), and a great light bursts through the east window, filling the chancel area; a new paschal candle is lit, and the proclamation of Easter faith fills the church: 'The light of Christ! Christos anesti! Christ is risen!' The congregation process into the chancel, gather around the altar, and celebrate the first Mass of Easter. The resurrection is heralded one more time.

Belief in the resurrection of Jesus is the cornerstone of Christian faith: 'On the third day, he rose again.' But do I believe it? Can I believe it? What does it mean, anyway? I grew up in a church where one couldn't possibly be a real Christian and ask such questions. And for years I never did ask them. I took it for granted that 'He rose again from the dead' meant simply that: one minute Jesus was dead, the next he was alive – end of argument. But as the years passed, the resurrection bothered me. I preached about it every Easter; reassured the doubting; repeated, interminably, the arguments that demonstrated that it had to be true. But increasingly, it bothered me.

The difficulty with questioning the resurrection is that it seems too important a thing to place in question. As Paul states: 'If Christ has not been raised, your faith is futile' (1 Cor. 15.17). It is the very epicentre of Christian faith; if we allow even the faintest shadow of doubt concerning this to enter our minds, there will be nothing left. So the doubts and questions are suppressed in a kind of 'silence of thought' that is far too often mistaken for faith. That is how it was for me for a long time. But then one day doubts and questions cluttered the back of my mind to such an extent that I had to deal with them – before they dealt with me!

I recall sitting in my office in our house in Clapham, allowing my imagination to go into the tomb where Jesus was laid. No one was there at the time, so imagination is all we have. Could I really believe that Jesus simply awoke? That he resuscitated, like someone coming-to out of a deep sleep? Did his eyes flicker, his body stretch, his hands clench as he looked around the chilly cave? I wasn't sure I could live with that scenario any more. There were too many questions. How did he get out of the grave clothes? What did he wear when he shed them? Did he borrow the gardener's overalls? Was that why Mary Magdalene mistook him for the gardener? Why was it only the disciples who saw him? After all, he was a well-known figure, so why didn't anyone else spot him moving around Jerusalem? Where did he hang out between his appearances to the disciples? Was he holed up in the Jerusalem caravan park, as one writer teasingly suggests?

With such conundrums harassing my imagination, I contemplated the more sceptical explanations. Was Jesus actually dead when they buried him, or was he simply in a state of deep unconsciousness from which he recovered in the cool atmosphere of the tomb? Was his body taken by the Romans and disposed of elsewhere? Some historians argue that all prisoners were generally buried by the Romans and not by friends or relatives, so could his remains have been dug up from a shallow grave by hungry animals and consumed? Was his resurrection an apparition or trance brought on by an altered state of consciousness in the disciples? Or, since the Gospels were written long after the event (Mark's, the earliest, was written around 65CE), were the resurrection accounts created by Christians to validate their belief that Jesus was indeed the Christ? Is the story of the resurrection essentially fictional?

Now, having thought about it for some years, I reject both extremes: I accept neither the highly literalized account of the resurrection defended by fundamentalists and conservative Christians, nor the rational explanations of the liberal sceptics. I believe in the resurrection as a real and cataclysmic event. But I see it as one that transcends any normal categories of understanding. It is an event that cannot be placed alongside any other event in human history. It is, quite simply, unique.

Before expanding on this critical affirmation of the resurrection, let's just clear the ground a little. To begin with, there were no eye-witnesses to the resurrection event itself. No one in the Bible claims to have been present when it happened. Whatever it was that occurred, it happened 'in the silence of God', as Ignatius put it. The silence and darkness of the tomb are impenetrable. All we have on the matter is conjecture. Also, the accounts in the Gospels of what happened outside the tomb and in the days that followed are fragmentary and inconsistent. They pose as many questions as they do answers.

Most importantly, it is very clear that Jesus was not simply resuscitated, as we are told Lazarus was, for example. This is a description of an entirely different phenomenon. A corpse does not come to life here and wait again to die. A body does not rise to bleed again. After the crucifixion, Jesus 'appeared' in places, the scriptures tell us. He did not walk through doorways. He did not travel as he did from Galilee to Jerusalem. He did not sail as he did to Capernaum. He did not ride by borrowed colt as he did on the way to the temple. He simply 'appeared' in the midst of people's lives, while they were doing mundane things, without warning but vividly, the same but different. 'No, the resurrection of Jesus is not about the revivification of an old life, it is about a new kind of life entirely.'[1]

So, do I believe in the bodily resurrection of Jesus? I'm afraid I have to give the immortal reply: it all depends on what you mean by 'bodily'. The best comment we have on this appears in 1 Corinthians 15, where Paul discusses the resurrection of the dead at length. Towards the end of the passage he makes it clear that he is talking about a mystery (v. 51) – something that transcends rational categories – so he uses a metaphor: the comparison with a seed falling into the ground and dying and then being reborn as a plant. 'What is sown is perishable, what is raised is imperishable', he says. 'It is sown a physical body, it is raised a spiritual body' (vv. 42–44). This is awkward and troubling language, but it is the only way Paul can discuss the subject.

Paul's letter to the Corinthians is significantly earlier than any of the Gospels – about a decade earlier than Mark's Gospel. And he says that his understanding was passed on to him from an earlier tradition. So Paul's description of the resurrection is by far the oldest in the New Testament. Interestingly, he makes no mention of an empty tomb, but majors instead on the aspect of Christ's appearances to his disciples, citing the testimonies that Christ had appeared to Peter, to the twelve, and then to 500 other followers. He then adds himself to the list (vv. 3–8). His own story is particularly useful since it gives a record of what he himself experienced when Christ appeared to him. He talks of 'seeing' the Lord, yet this seeing was clearly not an 'in the flesh' experience, but an inner encounter, a visionary experience of some kind. 'It pleased God through his grace to reveal his Son *in* me' (Gal. 1.15). And he makes no distinction between this encounter and that of the disciples. 'We ought probably to imagine that the women's experience of Christ at the tomb, and the disciples' experience in Galilee, as being not very different from this.'[2]

So what happened 'on the third day', and more importantly, how does it affect us today? Clearly, a transformation took place: the historical Jesus became the Christ of faith. He appeared to the disciples, but they all saw him differently now. Mary Magdalene failed to recognize him in the garden. The two disciples on the road to Emmaus walked several miles with him, engaging in deep discussion, and then sat around a table with him yet never realized who he was until the very end of the day – and only then through something he did rather than through his physical appearance. So this was no straightforward 'bodily' resurrection. 'He did not live with them now: he simply "came" to them', in strange yet glorious appearances. Yet the outcome of these appearances was utterly overwhelming in its impact on the disciples: they were transformed from fearful, defeated followers of a 'master' whom they believed to be dead into a dynamic community that literally changed the course of history.

What Mary Magdalene and the other disciples of Christ experienced was not an encounter with a resuscitated body that sat up, left the tomb and then walked about as it had before; rather, they experienced an eschatological event – 'an anticipation of eternal life for mortal beings.'[3] The risen Christ is the foreshadowing of a new creation, the firstfruits of a resurrected universe.[4] He was 'sown' a physical body and raised a 'spiritual' body, to use Paul's language. As Keith Ward, philosopher and theologian, argues: when Luke speaks of Jesus eating broiled fish, or when he cites Jesus reassuring his disciples that he was not a ghost (Luke 24.39, 42), he is not intending to convey Jesus' ordinariness or normal physicality, but his absolute extra-ordinariness:

This was not an ordinary physical body, which had presumably been hiding behind the door all the time, and had picked up some clothes from somewhere in Jerusalem. It was a totally extra-ordinary spiritual body, with the power to manifest itself when and where it chose, and to communicate nothing less than the divine life to those to whom it appeared. So it could indeed manifest in a body of flesh and bones, and eat fish ... It was not less than physical, like a spirit. It was more than physical, a complete transfiguration of the physical world into a greater spiritual reality, with the power to appear as a physical form for the sake of those who found it hard to believe such a transfiguration had happened or could happen.[5]

As to what happened to the physical body of Jesus, Ward argues that either it walked out, or 'it dematerialized, ceased to exist as a physical body of flesh and blood, being instantaneously transfigured into a different, spiritual form'.[6] On his account of things, Ward believes the latter. It is a line of thought he continues in his account of Christ's ascension into heaven, which is unintelligible if we think of a physical body soaring through the clouds to some distant galaxy, and then coming back like a rocket at some future time. The ascension makes sense, Ward argues, 'when we see Jesus' ascension as the final removal of his spiritual body from the physical realm, the final transfiguration of his material life into the life of eternity'.[7]

Some will find Ward's approach fanciful, and continue, instead, to see these stories as imaginative – yet, perhaps truthfull – attempts by the early Church to express the mystery that burst into their lives with the unexpected appearances of Christ after the crucifixion. Those who take such a view may still affirm the reality of the resurrection, albeit interpreted in a different way.

One thing is clear: Christians from different ends of the theological spectrum will argue incessantly about the form and historicity of the resurrection and the ascension of Christ. Yet little of this really impinges on our everyday lives in the twenty-first century. What matters now is not the actual form that the resurrection took, but the impact that the Spirit of the risen Christ has upon our lives today. Resurrection faith has two poles: one is historical and expresses a tradition of reports going back in time to the original tradition of apostolic appearances; and the other is the more immediate encounter with the presence of the risen Christ here and now. Our concern, then, should not be with rationalistic attempts to 'prove' a historical event that cannot in fact be substantiated by any means available to us today; but rather, with the experience of the living Christ in our lives and in our community.

Paul Ricoeur says that he is inclined to understand the resurrection as resurrection in the Christian community, which becomes the body of the living Christ. This is entirely consistent with the teaching of Paul in 1 Corinthians, where he plainly describes the Church as the body of Christ – the evidence of the resurrection (1 Cor. 12.27). Indeed, as Archbishop Peter Carnley points out, Paul locates the body of Christ in two places – 'on the altar and around the altar, as it were'.[8] For the bread of the Eucharist is said to be the body of Christ and the community that shares it is said also to be the body of Christ: 'The bread that we break, is it not a sharing in the body of Christ? ... we who are many are one body, for we all partake of the one bread' (1 Cor. 10.16–17).

As we look for the body of Christ, then, Paul directs us not to an empty tomb, but to the new location of Christ's body in the Church and in the sacrament of the Eucharist.

In a very real sense, the disciples' innocence was shattered at the cross. That was their moment of disenchantment: when Jesus died, hope died, a vision died, everything they believed in died. They were bereaved not only of a person they loved, but also of a dream. The resurrection, however, signalled the birth of a second innocence. Things would never go back to the way they were. They would never have Jesus living among them, as he once did. He reappeared, but not in the same familiar form. Jesus of Nazareth was gone. They couldn't turn the clock back to how things were. Yet out of this apparent loss and failure came a new life, better and stronger than it was before. And so it is with us. Faith must constantly die and be reborn. The process can be painful and unsettling, yet glorious.

'Believing in Christ's resurrection doesn't mean affirming a historical fact, and saying "Oh really?" It means being seized by the life-giving Spirit and experiencing "the powers of the world to come" (Heb. 6.5) in our own living and dying.'[9]

I believe in the resurrection of Christ. My faith is built on it – not on a theological conjecture as to what happened to a body of flesh and bone, but on the recognition that Christ is indeed alive in the world today. He lives in you and me. He lives in people. He lives in bread and wine, in kindness, in compassion, in justice, in laughter, in friendship, in goodness – wherever God's kingdom of life, hope and liberation is manifest, Christ is risen!

Notes

1 Joan Chittester, *In Search of Belief*, Hampshire: Redemptorist Publications, 1999, p. 133.

2 Jürgen Moltmann, *Jesus Christ for us Today*, London: SCM Press, 1994, p. 73f.

3 Moltmann, *Jesus Christ*, p. 242.

4 Keith Ward, *What the Bible Really Teaches*, London: SPCK, 2004, p. 120.

5 Ward, *What the Bible*, p. 123.

6 Ward, *What the Bible*, p. 121f.

7 Ward, *What the Bible*, p. 124.

8 Peter Carnley, *Reflections in Glass: Trends and Tensions in the Contemporary Anglican Church*, Sydney: HarperCollins, 2004, p. 119.

9 Jürgen Moltmann, *The Source of Life: The Holy Spirit and the Theology of Life*, London: SCM Press, 1997, p. 16.

9

May the Life Force be With You!

Receiving the motherly Spirit

Paul Ricoeur argues that it is by interpreting that we can believe again: re-enchantment is nurtured with fresh understanding, with fresh ways to *think* about the Christian faith. Yet there is more to it than this: re-enchantment also entails some kind of renewal of spirit: a fresh way to *feel* about the Christian faith. Re-enchanted Christianity is Spirited Christianity.

In recent times, talk of the Holy Spirit and of spiritual renewal has become virtually synonymous with the charismatic movement, with being 'filled with the Spirit' and exercising 'spiritual gifts' (*charismata*) like speaking in tongues, healing and prophecy. It is reported that almost half of all evangelical Christians worldwide are charismatics, and there is also a burgeoning charismatic movement within the Catholic Church: Pope John Paul II is reputed to have had a charismatic priest as his personal chaplain, though there is no evidence that he himself was a charismatic.

Most people involved with the charismatic movement affirm that their participation in it has reinvigorated their Christian lives. My own spiritual life was certainly reinvigorated by a charismatic experience during my mid-teens, when friends took me to a 'house church' meeting in an upper room of a large Victorian house in Liverpool. At the time, I was bored with church and only hanging on to faith by a thread. But I was intrigued by reports of what was going on at 'the house'. So I went along to see.

The meeting was like nothing I had ever encountered before. I was accustomed to worship that was restrained and predictable, yet what I witnessed there was anything but restrained and predictable. No one appeared to know what was going to happen next. People simply stood up whenever they felt prompted by the Holy Spirit and prayed or prophesied or struck up a chorus or spoke in tongues. It was all very spontaneous and chaotic, yet spiritually exciting. I loved it. So when an invitation was given for people to receive prayer and the laying on of hands to be 'filled with the Spirit', I was out of my seat like a shot. It's difficult to describe what happened next. When hands were laid on me I felt something like an electric current shooting through my body. I felt bathed in love. It was overwhelming. I laughed and cried and danced and fell to my knees and talked in tongues – all without the slightest sense of embarrassment or self-consciousness. I wasn't exactly out of control, but I wasn't entirely in control either.

This 'upper room' experience changed everything for me. When I turned up at my church a few days later, news of what had happened preceded me. It was a Brethren church, where things like speaking in tongues were thought to be of the devil, so the furrowed-browed elders gave me a choice: renounce it all, or leave the church – I was only seventeen! So I upped sticks and started attending meetings at 'the house'. During the early 1970s house churches were springing up all across the country, largely as a result of mainstream churches splitting over the charismatic experience. After a few years, I emerged as a national leader in the movement and, like everyone around me, believed that we were at the forefront of some great new work that God was doing.

Yet as time passed, doubts set in. I became uneasy with what I saw as a growing culture of certainty, characterized by emotional hype and bizarre phenomena, and with an underlying fundamentalist theology that I no longer identified with. By the late 1980s, twenty years after I became involved with charismatic churches, I arrived at the painful decision that I needed to move on.

All this seems a long time ago. I am now in an entirely different spiritual and theological environment. Yet I am thankful

77

for what the charismatic movement gave me, and I remain committed to what I call Spirited Christianity. Indeed, I see no future in the twenty-first century for expressions of Christianity that are not Spirited. Our postmodern world longs for numinosity: for a sense of awe and mystery, for sacredness, spirituality and enchantment, for something 'more' than the purely rational and cerebral. If the Church fails to engage with, and cater to this longing, it has no real future.

Clearly, for quite a lot of people, the charismatic movement offers an appealing form of Spirited Christianity; yet there are also lots of other people who are repelled by it, who choose to look for spiritual invigoration in other directions. Sacramental spirituality, for example, offers many disaffected charismatics a more satisfying expression of numinosity. When I asked a former house church colleague why he had shifted from a charismatic to an Anglo-Catholic church, he replied that it was the sense of mystery surrounding the Mass that attracted him. 'I love the whole sensory thing,' he said, 'the incense, the colour, the bells, the music, the lyrical words of the liturgy, the taste of bread and wine. It's a mixture of mystery and rootedness.' He is not alone: an increasingly well-worn path exists between the charismatic and the sacramental.

But there are other ways in which people experience numinosity or spiritedness. Some find it in silence, contemplation and meditative practices. Some discover it in art, in listening to Rachmaninov's 'Vespers', in singing along at a U2 gig, in climbing a hill or walking the dog, in sitting quietly in a beautiful building, or in any of a thousand other activities – none of which automatically evokes the numinous, yet all of which can.

What are we talking about? What do I mean by 'numinosity' or 'spiritedness'? Is it just a slightly spooky human sensation, or is it about something more? Does numinosity have anything to do with God?

In order to answer this, we need to think a little about pneumatology – the study of the person and work of the Holy Spirit (*pneuma* = breath, wind, spirit). I suppose it is not too surprising that most people's notion of the Holy Spirit revolves around what happened on the Day of Pentecost. It was, after all, the birthday of the Church, and one of the most dramatic occurrences in the New Testament, when the Spirit descended on the disciples with tongues of fire, transforming them from frightened individuals into an audacious community that changed the world. However, when God's Spirit is viewed mainly through the lens of Pentecost, the tendency is to colonize the Spirit's work within the Church, and to limit the Spirit's activities to certain special manifestations within the Christian community. The Spirit becomes the Spirit of the Church or the Spirit of faith, which is a serious distortion of who and what God's Spirit is about.[1]

Pneumatology begins not with Pentecost, but with the creation. Throughout the Old Testament, the Holy Spirit is revealed as *ruach* (the Hebrew word for Spirit), the holy breath or life-force of creation, the primal energy out of which creation evolves. In Genesis 1, the Spirit broods over the primordial chaos out of which creation evolves. Far from being simply the Spirit of the Church, God's Spirit is the Spirit of the cosmos, the breath of life in all that is. God unremittingly breathes the Spirit into creation, Jürgen Moltmann says:

> Everything that is, exists and lives in the unceasing inflow of the energies and potentialities of the cosmic Spirit. This means that we have to understand every created reality in terms of energy, grasping it as the realized potentiality of the divine Spirit. Through the energies and potentialities of the Spirit, the Creator is himself present in his creation. He does not merely confront it in his transcendence; entering into it, he is also immanent in it.[2]

God's Spirit is at the heart of everything, honouring no boundaries between the religious and the non-religious. The awe-inspiring sense of mystery that draws us towards something 'more', whether it be in a religious or non-religious context, emanates from the energies of the life-force, the divine *ruach*.

The Old Testament word *ruach* conveys something significantly different from the word 'spirit' and its Greek, Latin and Germanic equivalents (*pneuma, spiritus, Geist*/ghost), which are conceived as something antithetical to matter and body, where 'spirit' suggests something immaterial, disembodied, supersensory or supernatural. But to talk from a Hebrew context about Yahweh's *ruach* is to say: 'God is a tempest, a storm, a force in body and soul, humanity and nature.'[3] *Ruach* allows for no separation between spirit and body, between spirituality and sensuousness. Spirit is embodied in the world. Spirit animates creation. Spirit is the breath of all that breathes. If God withdraws his *ruach*, everything disintegrates into dust (Ps. 104.29). It is the breath of God's life that 'fills the world and holds together all things' (Wis. 1.7; Isa. 34.16). *Ruach* is the munificent, feminine life-force at the heart of everything.

Recognizing God's Spirit as the life-force, the holy breath of creation has vast implications for an ecological theology. Once God's Spirit is acknowledged as the Spirit of the cosmos, the animating energy within all things, then the material world matters – not as a mere resource for human consumption, or as an instrument of human will and purpose, but as the temple of the Spirit – the 'body of God', as theologian Sallie McFague puts it.[4] Creation is Spirited; suffused with divine presence. So it matters what we do to the world: it matters if we choke the atmosphere with CO_2 fumes, or if we pollute the soil with deadly chemicals, or if we destroy species and annihilate rainforests. It matters, not simply because we are blighting the earth for future human generations, but because the community of creation in all its creaturely diversity is precious and significant in its own right, because it is inhabited by the divine. In the words of the Nicaraguan poet and monk Ernesto Cardenal, creation is 'God's palpable, materialized love'.[5] Ecological responsibility is, therefore, not simply a matter of pragmatic wisdom, but a response to the presence of the life-giving Spirit in all things.

To describe the universe as being inundated or suffused with the divine Spirit is not pantheism – the concept of God being everything and everything being God. But rather, pan*en*theism (*pan* = everything; *en* = in; *theos* = God) – the affirmation that God is in everything and everything is in God. Panentheism does not reduce God to the universe: God is in everything, and everything is *in* God, but God is *more than* everything. A concise description of panentheism appears in the book of Acts where Paul tells the Athenians: 'In him we live and move and have our being' (Acts 17.28). God's Spirit is both the life-force of created beings and the living space in which they can grow and develop.[6] The famous inscription over the door to Carl Jung's house and on his tombstone, 'Bidden or not bidden, God is present', encapsulates a panentheistic outlook: invited or uninvited, recognized or unrecognized, the presence of God is here and everywhere.

Panentheism attempts to maintain a necessary tension between divine transcendence (God being entirely 'other than' creation), and divine immanence (God being present within creation). Too much stress on transcendence results in an absentee God 'out there', elsewhere, not here. On the other hand, an overemphasis on immanence leads to pantheism – God inseparably one with the material world, without any existence apart from it. A trinitarian approach to creation integrates transcendence and immanence: *God the Father* is the creating origin of creation, the divine 'other'; *God the Word* is its shaping origin, who also enters it becoming fully a part of it; *God the Mother Spirit* is its life-breathing origin, who permeates and sustains it as the life-force. Creation is 'from God, through God and in God'.[7]

The image of the Holy Spirit as God the Mother was quite familiar in the early years of Christianity, especially in Syria, but got lost in the patriarchal empire of Rome. As Moltmann says, if believers are 'born' of the Holy Spirit, then we have to think of the Spirit as the 'mother' of believers. And if the Spirit is the Comforter, the Paraclete, as John's Gospel declares, then she comforts as a mother comforts – 'the Spirit is the motherly comforter of her children'.[8]

The Spirit poured forth at Pentecost is unmistakably the

divine *ruach* – embodied in a noisy, rushing, violent wind that filled the house where the disciples were gathered, and in fiery tongues descending on the disciples' heads. Peter recognized what was happening as the fulfilment of the prophet Joel's words:

> In the last days it will be, God declares,
> that I will pour out my Spirit upon all flesh,
>   and your sons and your daughters shall prophesy,
> and your young men shall see visions,
>   and your old men shall dream dreams.
> Even upon my slaves, both men and women,
> in those days I will pour out my Spirit;
>   and they shall prophesy. (Acts 2.17–18)

Pentecost unleashed the wild, undomesticated Spirit of life indiscriminately on all flesh – on women as well as men, on old and young, slaves and free. Sweeping away the discrimination and prejudice of the ancient world, *ruach*, the divine Spirit, liberates people to become fully alive to who they are and who they can be.

Spirited Christianity began at Pentecost. This does not mean that we must have a dramatic Pentecostal experience. Spirited Christianity is Spirited *living* – following in the steps of Jesus, a human being full of life and passion and alive to every new possibility, fully self-aware yet not self-possessed, affirming life yet willing to sacrifice it, honouring tradition but not bound by convention, given to all yet possessed by none.

Jesus breathed on his disciples after his resurrection, saying, 'Receive the Holy Spirit.' Yet he had been breathing Holy Breath into people throughout his life and ministry. He breathed hope into the downcast and the dejected, justice into the oppressed, love into the unloved. He breathed acceptance into the outcast. He breathed freedom into those bound by fear. He breathed joy, friendship, adventure, wisdom, peace and colour into what is often a sad, painful, lonely, hopeless grey world.

Spirited Christianity means waking up on the inside, becoming fully alive. It is about sensing the life-force of the divine Spirit in the present moment. It is about saying 'Yes' to life in spite of its difficulties, frustrations and disappointments. It is about living life in the Spirit of Jesus. It is about breathing in life, hope and liberation, and then breathing them out on to others. To be Spirited is to have vitality.

The Holy Spirit, God's energizing presence among us, the life force that drives us beyond ourselves, that whispers us into the great quest within, that makes life alive with a purpose not seen but deeply, consciously, stubbornly felt even in the midst of chaos, even at the edge of despair, sounds the truth in us that we are more than we seem to be. Life does not begin and end with us. There is more than we know, there is an electric charge animating the world at every level and, most of all, within. Holy Spirit suffuses all of life, calls us into the mystery that is God, reminds us of the model that is Jesus, brings us into the fullness of ourselves. Holy Spirit is the great anti-gravitational force that calls us out of somewhere into everywhere, that keeps us moving toward, through, the black holes of life, certain that on the other side of them is light, waiting and wishing us on.[9]

Notes

1 Jürgen Moltmann, *The Spirit of Life: A Universal Affirmation*, London: SCM Press, 1992, p. 8.

2 Jürgen Moltmann, *God in Creation: An Ecological Doctrine of Creation*, London: SCM Press, 1985, p. 9.

3 Moltmann, *The Spirit*, p. 40.

4 Sallie McFague, *The Body of God: An Ecological Theology*, London: SCM Press, 1993.

5 Quoted in Moltmann, *The Spirit*, p. 211.

6 Jürgen Moltmann, *The Source of Life: The Holy Spirit and the Theology of Life*, London: SCM Press, 1997, p. 71.

7 Moltmann, *God in Creation*, p. 98.

8 Moltmann, *The Source*, p. 35.

9 Joan Chittester, *In Search of Belief*, Hampshire: Redemptorist Publications, 1999, p. 162.

10

A Spirituality of Belonging

Feeling at home in the world

Rachel visited London a couple of times a year in connection with her work. She mostly stayed at our house, where we invariably engaged in long conversations well into the night, generally consuming more red wine than we should. Rachel had long ago dismissed religion, but she was a spirited soul with a zest for life and a passion for justice. We shared a lot in common, despite our different views about God. However, in one conversation, at about 2.30am, she seemed concerned that our views may be converging a little too much. Sipping nervously on her wine she said, 'But you need to remember, Dave: I *am* an atheist.' With a wry smile, I said, 'Maybe Rachel, but you are a very spiritual atheist.' 'Oh yes, of course,' she replied without a moment's hesitation, giving the impression that she would have been insulted for me to think otherwise.

Religion and spirituality are no longer presumed to be bedfellows. Many people baulk at theistic religion yet nevertheless believe that life consists in more than the purely material. Religionless spirituality is in fact now commonplace. The point was underscored for me a couple of years ago when leading a university mission in Cambridge. One afternoon I found myself chatting with a dozen or so students in a bar, none of whom had any religious affiliations, but most of whom had an interest in spirituality. As the discussion progressed, I asked them what they thought about Christian spirituality. 'Christian spirituality?', one of them mused; 'I don't think I've ever thought of putting those two words together.' In his mind,

Christianity had to do with beliefs, doctrines, creeds and rituals, but not spirituality. And he is not alone.

Contrary to mid-twentieth-century predictions, we do not live in a totally secularized society. Many people outside formal religion feel that their life has been touched by the transcendent; many search for spiritual meaning and wisdom. However, it is a quest that tends not to lead people to the Church or to Christianity. They are looking for a spiritual path to follow, not a belief system, but it is the belief system they associate with the Church and not the spiritual path. So they look elsewhere.

But many people in the Church feel the same way; many regular churchgoers long for a living spirituality. A cursory glance around most religious bookshops will demonstrate the point: any number of books is available on this or that aspect of spirituality. There is a hunger for spiritual guidance, for spiritual resources, both within and beyond church communities. I have no doubt that the future of the Church in Western societies hinges on its ability to engage with and cater for this spiritual hunger. Churches that fail to engage heart as well as head, or which fail to ignite the imagination, or which fail to help people to find meaning in their lives, are unsustainable in the twenty-first century: people long for a sense of mystery in their lives, for manifestations of the numinous, for enchantment, for spirit. Churches need to be Spirited communities if they wish to avoid extinction.

In 1977 the Scottish Churches Council defined Christian spirituality in terms that still sound remarkably contemporary and relevant. It talked about spirituality as 'an exploration into what is involved in becoming human', and described 'becoming human' as 'an attempt to grow in sensitivity to self, to others, to the non-human creation, and to God who is within and beyond this totality'.[1] Christian spirituality is not primarily a 'religious' affair, or a situation of 'me and God', but rather the pursuit of true humanity through a growing sensitivity to the relational complex of which we are a part, which includes other people, the natural world, God and ourselves.

I believe that the spirituality for which many yearn is a spirituality of belonging: of belonging to a human community, of belonging to the family of creation, of belonging in the cosmos, of belonging in their bodies. 'The Western imagination has become alienated from the sacred mystery of life, alienated from its numinous source. Western culture has become spiritless, a culture of estrangement, a culture in which more and more people are living as strangers to their own being.'[2] We need a fresh understanding of what it means to be spirited creatures embodied in a material world. We need a fresh sense of belonging. Christianity at its best can cater to this need. When Archbishop William Temple famously said that 'Christianity is the most materialistic religion in the world', he was not referring to the wealth of the Vatican but to the fact that Christianity has the highest regard for matter and for the material world. Christian spirituality is in its very essence a spirituality of belonging, of spirit wedded to matter – not least, because the central affirmation of Christianity is that the divine became fully embodied in the person of Jesus Christ.

Yet all too often, the Christian spirituality we encounter is more of a spirituality of alienation than one of belonging. The dominating metaphor is that of exile: Christians are exiled on earth, longing for the homeland of heaven. This is the kind of Christianity that millions of people have turned their backs on. The story goes a bit like this:

Imagine the world as a kind of cosmic motel on the road to heaven. The motel is a very beautiful place; after all, God did originally create it, and it still bears the marks of his creation in its design and construction and in its lush surrounding gardens, the countryside. However, God's archenemy, satan, has managed to take possession of the place, which is now rat-infested and filthy. As a result, the future of the motel is strictly limited: soon after we depart, it will be completely demolished. In the meantime, we continue to live here, patiently and joyfully looking forward to the big departure to our real home in God's mansion far down the road. We are warned not to unpack our bags in the motel, or get attached to our rooms, or worse still enjoy the leisure facilities too much, but to remember that we have a job to do: to warn other guests about the motel's impending doom, and to encourage them also to be prepared for a hasty getaway once the heavenly bus arrives, or perish with the motel.

Historically, much of the spirituality of alienation in Christianity can be traced back to Gnostic influences in the early centuries of the church – influences that have proved deeply resilient within the Western branches of the Church. By demonizing matter and the material world, Gnosticism radically challenged the Judeo-Christian vision of the world's goodness. Gnostics saw spirit as good, and matter as evil: the human being was trapped in the corruption of the physical body. So earthly things – the body and sexual appetites in particular – were considered bad. Salvation, according to the Gnostics, was to be freed from the physical realm, in order to return to the realm of pure spirit.

Throughout the history of the Church, from Clement of Alexandria and Origen through Augustine and down to the present day, Gnostic dualism between spirit and matter has characterized much, maybe most, of Christianity; 'Christian orthodoxy has never really rid itself of the gnostic influence.'[3] The outcome has been a basic mistrust of the body and bodily desires, and a sense of dislocation from the material world, which is a place simply to journey through.

This fundamental breach between the physical and the spiritual has proven disastrous at a pastoral level. Sam Keen, the noted American author and professor of philosophy and religion, expressed the problem perfectly, more than thirty years ago:

What has happened to me? How am I to understand this warmth and grace which pervades my body? As I begin to reflect, I realize that neither the Christian nor the secular culture, in which I have been jointly nurtured, have given me adequate categories to interpret such an experience. Neither has taught me to discern the sacred in the voice of the body and the language of the senses. In the same measure that Christian theology has failed to help me appreciate the *carnality of grace*, secular ideology has failed to provide me categories for understanding the *grace of carnality*. Before I can understand what I have experienced, I must see where Christian theology and secular ideology have failed me.[4]

Body–soul dualism is foreign to the Jewish world-view, foreign to the Old Testament, the Hebrew scriptures. To be quintessentially Jewish was and is to have a voracious appetite for life in all its material and physical reality. 'Eat heartily and drink your wine lustily', writes the author of Ecclesiastes (9.7). And there is an old Jewish saying that advises, 'A person will have to give account on the judgement day of every good thing which he or she refused to enjoy when they might have done so.'[5]

Yet from its earliest days, two strands of spirituality have existed side by side in Christianity, offering quite different accounts of the material and bodily world.[6] The one that has predominated in the Western Church is based on a vision of the human spirit rising above the natural, physical or material world in order to commune with God in the 'spiritual' realm. From this perspective the mundane world must be transcended and earthly things shunned as impediments to spiritual growth and progress. A clear distinction is drawn between the 'sacred' and the 'secular', between 'piety' and 'worldliness'. Augustine offers the paradigmatic expression of this strand of spirituality when he writes: 'I desire to have knowledge of God and the soul. Of nothing else? No, of nothing else whatsoever.'[7]

The second strand strongly rejects the idea that we must escape the world in order to commune with God. In this approach to Christianity the presence of the divine is celebrated within the physical and material realm; human embodiment is greeted with joy and gratitude. The expectation is to encounter God within both the world of nature, and the world of human culture and human experience. St Francis offers a paradigmatic expression of this strand of spirituality when, as he was about to die, in that most intimate moment of communion with God, he kept reciting his elegant 'Canticle to the Sun', that placed him in solidarity with the birds, the insects, the sun and the moon, and indeed the whole world of nature. For St Francis, God was a present reality in the physical world.[8]

There are no prizes for guessing which of these strands of spirituality I personally identify with. But what do we do with the first strand? The image of ascent within Christian spirituality is widespread, as also are the themes of restlessness in this life, and exile and longing for 'home'. Is there any meeting point for the two approaches?

I think that the best way to reconcile the strands of homelessness and belonging in Christian tradition lies in the notion of a cosmic adventure. Science has increasingly, almost reluctantly, adopted the perception of the cosmos as story. Through the science of cosmology the universe has increasingly become a narrative, a great adventure. Over the past century and more, starting from the Darwinian story of life on planet earth, a scientific vision has emerged moving back in time to embrace the astrophysical origins of the cosmos fifteen or twenty billion years ago. 'The most expressive metaphor for what science finds in nature today is no longer *law*, but *story*.'[9]

Christian theology also incorporates a story of the cosmos, beginning with the creation myths in Genesis, and concluding with an eschatological vision of the future. The sense of alienation from the world, and of unease with physicality and carnality found in some aspects of Christian tradition, stems from a particular eschatological vision in which only the human spirit has eternal significance; the natural world has no future. Yet there are many indications to the contrary in scripture. In particular, Paul's comments in Romans 8 suggest a cosmic adventure for the whole of creation (Rom. 8.19–23). The entire created order waits with eager anticipation to be 'set free from its bondage to decay', Paul says. The groans of creation are the groans of labour pain, the anticipation of a new birth, not the grunts of terminal disease. The vision in Romans 8 is not that of humans inheriting God's future purposes while the material world is destroyed and dispensed with, but rather it is a vision of humanity and creation journeying together into the fullness of God's eternal purpose. The world, therefore, is not a mere departure point for a human journey, but a fellow traveller into the deep mystery of God's eternity.

A spirituality of belonging is rooted in the reality of the incarnation – God becoming enfleshed, living among us and sharing fully in what it means to be creaturely. And in the symbolism of his ascension, Christ takes humanity and the whole of creation into the very heart of God. The sense of both rootedness and restlessness are celebrated in the Eucharist, the core Christian ritual. When we share bread and wine around the table of Christ we celebrate divine embodiment, the feast of heavenly love revealed in flesh and blood, and sharing in the pain and suffering of the world. We also affirm that the divine Spirit is mediated through the physical and the material. The offertory prayer uttered by the priest as he or she gives thanks for the elements of bread and wine expresses this point exquisitely:

> Blessed are you, Lord God of all creation; through your goodness we have this bread to offer, which earth has given and human hands have made. It will become for us the bread of life.

The Eucharist not only celebrates the love of God revealed in Christ, but also declares boldly that both the natural creation and the realm of human endeavour can bear the divine. As we partake of bread and wine we seek no flight from the world of mundane things, the world of friends and strangers, of bodily senses and carnal appetites, of hopes and aspirations, disappointments and fears. Rather, we bring the entire universe of creation to the table to share in the great thanksgiving for the gift of life and the new creation in Christ.

It would be perfectly fitting to conclude the eucharistic prayer with the very Jewish exclamation from *Fiddler on the Roof*: 'To life! To life! L'chaim!' For the Eucharist is nothing less than a full-blooded celebration of life in all its abundance and diversity.

In an ecological age when we recognize what appalling damage we are causing the earth by treating it as mere matter, an instrument of human will and purpose, we desperately need a spirituality of belonging, a sense of kinship with the planet and with the whole family of creation rooted in the affirmation that the universe lives by the energy of the divine Spirit and shares in the eternal adventure of God's loving purpose. And in a world of anguish and injustice, we need to sense our deep connectedness with all people, especially with those whose lives are overshadowed by pain and suffering, by tyranny and inequality, by oppression, hunger and poverty. If we belong to the earth, we belong to the peoples of the earth. To eat the bread and drink the wine of the Eucharist without accepting a loving responsibility to the care of others is to miss the whole point of the sacred feast.

Frankly, I am fed up with 'other worldly' Christian spirituality, with the piety that leaves people feeling alienated from their own selves, their bodies, and from the physical world of nature. I have had enough of the guilt-inducing religion that makes a misery of lives and fails monumentally to celebrate the gift of life. I want to stand on God's good earth and know I belong. I believe in a God who inhabits bodies, who is comfortable with human passion, who dances to the rhythms of nature and feels the beat of a lover's heart, who feasts on friendship and drinks to the health of our planet, who sees the plight of the poor and needy and never says, 'There, there. You will be all right when you get to heaven.'

> Be praised, O Lord, through our sister Mother Earth,
> For she sustains and guides our life,
> And yields us diverse fruits, with coloured flowers, and grass.[10]

Take a moment to sense your own groundedness in the physical world. Place your feet flat on the ground. Rest your hands on your knees. Open yourself to the energizing life-force of God's Spirit, the breath of the universe. Follow your own breath deep down into your belly. Make the connection.

Dear God, we pray for another way of being; another way of knowing. Across the difficult terrain of our existence we have attempted to build a highway and in so doing have lost our footpath. God, lead us to our footpath: lead us there where in simplicity we may move at the speed of natural creatures and feel the earth's love beneath our feet. Lead us there where step by step we may feel the movement of creation in our hearts. And lead us there where side by side we may feel the embrace of the common soul. Nothing can be loved at speed. God, lead us to the slow path; to the joyous insights of the pilgrim; another way of knowing: another way of being. Amen.[11]

Notes

1 Quoted in Sallie McFague, *Super, Natural Christians*, London: SCM Press, 1997, p. 10.

2 Robert Hamilton, *Earthdream: The Marriage of Reason and Intuition*, Bideford, Devon: Green Books, 1990, p. 179.

3 Kenneth Leech, 'The Carnality of Grace: Sexuality, Spirituality and Pastoral Ministry', in James Woodward (ed.), *Embracing the Chaos: Theological Responses to AIDS*, London: SPCK, 1990, p. 59.

4 Sam Keen, *To a Dancing God: Notes of a Spiritual Traveller*, San Francisco: HarperCollins, 1991, p. 142.

5 Quoted in Alec R. Vidler, *Essays in Liberality*, London: SCM Press, 1957, p. 99.

6 H. Paul Santmire, *The Travail of Nature: The Ambiguous Ecological Promise of Christian Theology*, Philadelphia: Fortress Press, 1985, p. 9.

7 Quoted in Santmire, *The Travail*, p. 9.

8 For a fuller explanation of these two approaches to Christian spirituality, see Santmire, *The Travail*.

9 John F. Haught, 'Religious and Cosmic Homelessness: Some Environmental Implications', in Charles Birch, William Eakin and Jay B. McDaniel (eds), *Liberating Life: Contemporary Approaches to Ecological Theology*, New York: Orbis Books, 1990, pp. 159–81.

10 From 'The Canticle of the Sun' by Francis of Assisi.

11 Michael Leunig, *When I Talk To You: A Cartoonist Talks To God*, Sydney: HarperCollins, 2004.

II

The Illogic of Hell

Will God restore all things in the End?

It is reported that Lloyd George, the early twentieth-century British prime minister, once said:

> When I was a boy the thought of heaven used to frighten me more than the thought of hell. I pictured heaven as a place where there would be perpetual Sundays, with perpetual services from which there would be no escape, as the Almighty, assisted by cohorts of angels, would always be on the lookout for those who did not attend.

I can identify with this. Hell never frightened me as a lad; it was always heaven that bothered me! Actually, growing up in a strong Christian home, it never even crossed my mind that I might end up 'downstairs'. However, the thought of praying and singing hymns for all eternity struck my young mind as a form of everlasting torment in itself.

Despite the confidence with which some Christians seem able to talk about heaven and hell and the eternal destiny of humankind, the reality is that none of us knows what lies ahead: whether eternal life is true or not, whether hell exists, whether there is anything at all beyond this life. The sum total of all that we can say on the subject amounts to nothing more than 'stammering in the face of impenetrable mysteries'.[1]

And yet Christians do talk about the afterlife all the time, sometimes in ways that are far from 'stammering'. I was told recently about the funeral of a stillborn child that took place in a fundamentalist church in central London. After the service a member of the congregation inquired of the curate what he thought the eternal fate of the baby might be. With all the compassion and self-assurance of a psychopath, the curate replied: 'She's gone straight to hell!'

The cluster of questions that surrounds the subject of death and the afterlife is intriguing, and explain why some people are so powerfully attracted to religion, and others are so vigorously repelled. The notion of hell, of everlasting torment, is the point at which many people's faith starts to unravel. There are lots of things within Christianity that the rational mind might baulk at, but the idea of a loving God despatching people to eternal misery for not believing the Christian message, or for belonging to a different faith community, or whatever, appears utterly incredible to most people in the twenty-first century. Without this doctrine being dumped or radically reinterpreted, re-enchantment with Christianity appears impossible.

Yet there is another question that precedes the issue of heaven and hell, which is: how can we be sure that there is anything at all after death? Frankly, I have to say that I don't know. I haven't died yet. I can quote Bible verses on the subject, recite traditional Christian beliefs and tell you what I think, but like everyone else on this earth, I only have faith, hope and speculation on the matter.

Developments over recent years in the research of near-death experiences certainly offer intriguing food for thought on the question of life after death. 'Near-death experiences', a term coined by Dr Raymond Moody in the late 1970s, are the perceptions reported by people who nearly died or who were clinically dead, then revived. Such experiences are now recognized to be very common, especially since the development of cardiac resuscitation techniques; about one-fifth of those who revive from clinical death claim to have had such an experience.

Actually, the earliest reference to a near-death experience (NDE) goes back much further that the 1970s, to Plato's *Republic*, written in the fourth century BC, which tells of a soldier who suffers a near-fatal injury on the battlefield being revived in the funeral parlour and describing a journey from darkness to light by guides, also a moment of judgement, feelings of peace and joy, and visions of extraordinary beauty and happiness.[2] There are other similar historical descriptions of NDEs. However, the prevalence of them in recent times is linked, as I say, to modern resuscitation procedures, which quite literally bring people back to life.

Dr Sam Parnia, a British doctor working in critical care medicine in New York's Cornell University, and a leading researcher in the field, identifies the following common features of the typical NDE:

- Feelings of peace.
- Seeing a bright light.
- Seeing a tunnel.
- Meeting departed relatives.
- Arriving at a new heavenly domain.
- Looking down on one's own body.
- A life review.
- Encountering a mystical being.[3]

Generally, those who undergo an NDE also report that it had a profound effect upon their life, causing them to question their values and relationships in positive ways.

The main question behind NDEs, however, is whether they offer evidence that the mind can exist apart from the brain, which would then support the possibility of conscious life beyond death. A BBC 2 documentary entitled *The Day I Died*, featuring Dr Parnia and the eminent neuro-psychiatrist Peter Fenwick, certainly left me thinking that such evidence is very close. Prior to watching that programme I had assumed that such experiences probably had chemical or psychological explanations. Dr Fenwick offered convincing arguments against that assumption.

One particularly striking story on the programme related to an American woman who underwent very tricky brain surgery to remove a tumour from her brain stem. The procedure required that all brain activity be suspended. She needed to be dead, to all intent and purpose. Yet despite her total absence of brain activity, the woman later described in detail things that were said and done in the operating theatre. She also experienced all the classic elements of an NDE. She spoke of arriving in a place of brilliant light, where she asked her uncle, who had died years before, if the light was God. He replied that 'the light is what happens when God breathes'. He then told her that she must return. She objected, saying that she wanted to stay. He said: 'What about your children? They need you.' She said, 'Oh they'll be fine!' The surgeon performing the operation confirmed that there was no physiological explanation for the woman being able to describe his procedures or recollect detailed conversations in the operating theatre.

If conscious perception can, even momentarily, be separated from the body, the assumed linkage between consciousness and the brain is placed in question, leaving the issue of life beyond death wide open. Scientists still require further evidence on the matter. Yet as Dr Parnia says, 'We now have the technology and scientific knowledge to explore the ultimate question.' Watch this space.

Of course, the outcome of such research will be a matter of indifference to those Christians who are convinced that they already know what lies beyond the grave. For such people it is all very clear cut: when we die we will face divine judgement. If we have believed the gospel of Christ and accepted salvation through his redeeming work on the cross, we will be received into everlasting bliss in heaven. If, on the other hand, we have not accepted that message or if we have failed to place our faith in Christ, we will spend eternity in hell in unending torment.

If one is exposed to that sort of message constantly, as I was in my childhood, it is amazing how anaesthetized one can become to its grotesque nature. The injustice of it all is absurd. Yes, of course there are some deeply malevolent people in the world whom we may think deserve to suffer great pain and torment, but can it really be right that people suffer such a fate for not believing in God or accepting the Christian gospel?

It is surely a ludicrous and inhuman idea, completely unworthy of a God of love and grace. Yes, I know God is also a righteous God, but what can be righteous or just about eternal suffering?

This vision of hell as everlasting torment arises from a literalistic reading of passages in the Bible that are clearly metaphorical. Parables in the New Testament, for example, that speak of wheat and tares, and of casting the tares onto a fiery rubbish dump, or of casting unworthy servants into 'outer darkness', are vivid warnings about judgement, but they are not to be taken literally. A major root source of the idea of everlasting hell-fire is the word *gehenna* – one of the words translated as 'hell' in English Bibles. The name derives from the burning rubbish dump just outside Jerusalem, which burned non-stop, day and night. This became metaphorically identified with the entrance to the underworld of punishment in the afterlife. The Islamic word for hell, *Jahannam*, comes from the same source.

However, things are changing. Belief in everlasting punishment is in decline in many parts of the Western Church. One report from the Church of England's Doctrine Commission concludes that the shift away from the notion of everlasting punishment amounts to one of the most notable transformations of Christian belief in modern times – a point underlined by a spate of books by conservative authors who find the demise of hell-fire teaching an 'unsettling development'.

One widely adopted alternative view to eternal punishment is that of 'annihilation' or 'total non-being', which simply says that those who reject God's love will cease to exist. C. S. Lewis offers one of the most persuasive versions of this approach in *The Great Divorce*, an engaging fictionalization of what happens when we die.

According to Lewis, hell is not a place that God sends people to who fail to believe the gospel, but a state of being one chooses to adopt or to become. 'Hell was not made for men', Lewis writes. 'It is in no sense *parallel* to heaven.' It is the 'darkness outside, the outer rim where being fades away into nonentity'.[4] To walk in the direction of a heavenly state is to become truly alive; to progress towards a hellish state is to fade into non-being. So when we describe someone as inhuman, we are acknowledging that they are dying on the inside, sinking into un-life.

Freedom of choice is very important in Lewis's approach. He viewed human beings as being on a road in life, progressing towards a state of either heaven or hell. Each moral choice we make takes us further along that road and slowly changes us into a more heavenly or more hellish creature. He writes:

> Every time you make a choice you are turning the central part of you, the part that chooses, into something a little different from what it was before. And taking your life as a whole, with all your innumerable choices, all your life long you are slowly turning this central thing either into a heavenly creature or into a hellish creature: either into a creature that is in harmony with God, and with other creatures, and with itself, or else into one that is in a state of war and hatred with God, and with its fellow-creatures, and with itself ... Each one of us at each moment is progressing to the one state or the other.[5]

The good news according to Lewis's understanding is that God is totally committed to reconcile everyone to becoming heavenly creatures. And there is no reason to believe that this redeeming process ceases at death. With an intriguing reinterpretation of the Catholic doctrine of purgatory, Lewis believes that God continues to offer grace to people beyond the grave.[6]

The Great Divorce is an imaginative portrayal of people still deciding after death which kind of people they wish to be. In the story, hell is depicted as a dismal city populated with self-righteous people, who see no need of God's help. But everyone is invited to visit heaven on a red bus that makes the journey each day. Once there, they can choose to stay or return. One man who rushes back to the bus as soon as he arrives in the outer reaches of heaven is convinced that there was a mistake. A former employee who was convicted of murder meets him in heaven. 'What I'd like to understand', he blurts, 'is what you're here for, as pleased as Punch, you, a bloody murderer, while I've been walking the streets down there and living in a place like a pigsty all these years.' The former employee admits his sin and tries to explain God's grace, but the other man wants none of it. He feels that a great injustice has been done. 'I'd rather be damned than go along with you,' he says. 'If they're too fine to have me without you, I'll go home.' He gets back on the bus.[7]

Lewis believed that, by God's grace, the gates of heaven are eternally open; God wills that none should perish. The doors of hell are locked on the inside, he insists. In *The Great Divorce*, some people take up the offer of God's grace, but others continue to resist it.

The Mystery of Salvation, a report by the Doctrine Commission of the Church of England, published in 1995, follows a similar annihilationist route. 'Hell is not eternal torment', it says, but rather, 'the final and irrevocable choosing of that which is opposed to God so completely and absolutely that the only end is total non-being.' The report spurns imagery of hell-fire, eternal torment and punishment, which it says has been used to frighten people into believing, and in the process 'left searing psychological scars on many'. The reason for the shift away from the notion of everlasting punishment in recent times, it says, has been 'the moral protest from both within and without the Christian faith against a religion of fear, and a growing sense that the picture of a God who consigned millions to eternal torment was far removed from the revelation of God's love in Christ'.[8]

According to *The Mystery of Salvation* hell is 'the ultimate affirmation of the reality of human freedom'. In other words, if God has created us with freedom, the option ultimately to reject God's offer of eternal life must be present.

In an essay entitled 'The Logic of Hell',[9] Jürgen Moltmann offers an alternative view to annihilation, rooted in a belief in 'universal reconciliation' or 'the restoration of all things' – a doctrine that traces back to early Church Fathers like Clement of Alexandria, Origen, Gregory of Nyssa and Gregory of Nazianzen, and also to the New Testament itself where Paul speaks of God reconciling to himself all things in Christ, and ultimately being all in all.

Freedom of choice is intrinsic to belief in hell, Moltmann argues; it is the main principle behind 'the logic of hell'. The story goes a bit like this: although God's love has reached out to us, plumbing the uttermost depths of hell, the possibility remains for each human of a final rejection of God, and so of eternal life. So human freedom overrides God's eternal purpose. Moltmann takes issue with this 'logic of hell', the supremacy of individual human will and choice.

First and foremost, to make human freedom paramount is inhumane, Moltmann claims, because most people cannot enjoy that freedom with respect to their eternal fate. What happens to people who never had the choice or the power to decide – the children who died early, the severely handicapped, the people suffering from geriatric diseases? Are they in heaven, or in total non-being, or somewhere between, in a limbo? What about the billions of people whom the gospel never reached and who were never faced with the choice? What happens to the Jews, or indeed members of other faith communities who cannot believe in Christ? Are they all destined for annihilation? And what of the earth and the whole family of creation, which the Creator after all found to be 'very good'? Are they too to disappear into non-being? The obvious outcome of the 'logic' of freedom of human choice is that in the end not many are going to be with God in heaven. Most will be fated to eternal annihilation – which is certainly better than eternal torment, but still profoundly unjust. Perhaps this logic of hell is an illusion, Moltmann concludes, this presupposition that it all depends on the human being's free will.

But the logic of hell is not only inhumane in Moltmann's view; it is also basically atheistic, in that human freedom of choice, human will, finally prevails. 'God is merely the accessory who puts that will into effect. If I decide for heaven, God must put me there; if I decide for hell, he has to leave me there.'[10] The logic of hell is to make human choice the supreme decider.

Make no mistake: hell exists, in Moltmann's understanding of things, not as a place, but as an existential reality in human experience. The twentieth century produced more infernos than all the centuries before: the gas chambers of Auschwitz and the atomizing of Hiroshima heralded an age of potential mass annihilation. 'So many people have experienced hells! It is pointless to deny hell. It is a possibility that is constantly round about us and within us.'[11]

In this context, the gospel of Christ's descent into hell is particularly relevant, Moltmann says: Christ suffered the 'inescapable remoteness from God', and the 'God-forsakenness' that knows no way out, so that he could bring God to the God-forsaken. 'Christ brought hope to the place where according to Dante all who enter must "abandon hope".'[12] The New Testament image is of Christ in his death descending to the deepest, most hellish depths of God-forsakenness that humanity can experience, and leading the captives out of hell into the hope and freedom in God's love in the new creation. 'The true Christian foundation for the hope of universal salvation is the theology of the cross, and the realistic consequence of the theology of the cross can only be the restoration of all things.'[13]

God is committed to reconciling to himself all things, on earth and in heaven (Col. 1.21). 'God will be all in all' (1 Cor. 15.28).

'There can be no question of God's giving up anything or anyone in the whole world, either today or in all eternity. The end has to be: Behold, everything is God's!'[14] Divine judgement can only be welcomed: a point at which the mangled mess of human history will be sorted. This will certainly stir up excruciating regret. But judgement is not God's last word.

Judgment establishes in the world the divine righteousness on which the new creation is to be built. But God's last word is 'Behold, I make all things new' (Rev. 21.5). From this no one and nothing is excepted. Love is God's compassion with the lost. Transforming grace is God's punishment for sinners.[15]

Ultimately, no one in this life knows what happens when we die. Like Moltmann, I cannot proclaim with certainty that everyone will be redeemed, but I share his trust that 'the proclamation will go forward until everyone has been redeemed'.[16]

Notes

1 Peter Berger, *Questions of Faith*, Oxford: Blackwell Publishing, 2004, p. 173.

2 Sam Parnia, *What Happens When We Die? A Ground-Breaking Study into the Nature of Life and Death*, London: Hay House, 2005, p. 15.

3 Quoted from a lecture by Drs Sam Parnia and Peter Fewick at the University of Southampton, 15 May 2001, available at <www.Culture-Watch.org>.

4 C. S. Lewis, *The Problem of Pain*, London: Geoffrey Bles: The Centenary Press, 1940, p. 115.

5 C. S. Lewis, *Mere Christianity*, Glasgow: Collins, 1987, p. 83.

6 See, for example, C. S. Lewis, *Letters to Malcolm Chiefly on Prayer*, London: Geoffrey Bles: The Centenary Press, 1964, pp. 137–43 (chapter 20).

7 C. S. Lewis, *The Great Divorce*, Glasgow: Collins, 1972, p. 30ff.

8 *The Mystery of Salvation: The Story of God's Gift*, London: Church House Publishing, 1995, p. 198f.

9 Jürgen Moltmann, 'The Logic of Hell', in Richard Bauckham (ed.), *God Will Be All in All: The Eschatology of Jürgen Moltmann*, Edinburgh: T. & T. Clark, 1999, p. 43f.

10 Moltmann, 'The Logic', p. 45.

11 Moltmann, 'The Logic', p. 46.

12 Moltmann, 'The Logic', p. 46.

13 Jürgen Moltmann, *The Coming of God: Christian Eschatology*, London: SCM Press, 1996, p. 251.

14 Christoph Blumhardt, quoted in Moltmann, 'The Logic', p. 47.

15 Moltmann, *The Coming*, p. 251.

16 Moltmann, *Jesus Christ for Today's World*, London, SCM Press, 1994, p. 143.

12

Re-Spiriting Church

Mystery, magic and liberating ritual

It is just after eight o'clock on a weekday evening in a busy south London pub where a few friends and I have organized an unusual worship service. The upstairs 'function' room is packed with people mainly in their twenties or early thirties, most of whom are holding a pint of beer or sipping a glass of wine.

The room is lit by dozens of small candles. There is a large projected image of Rublev's icon of the Holy Trinity at the far end of the room, and a number of other projected icons are displayed on the other walls. Montage sequences of people embracing are projected onto a large sheet hanging in the centre of the room. There is also a triptych comprised of three gothic-shaped panels, each covered haphazardly with pieces of broken mirror. In front of the triptych are several small cushions and a bowl of scented oil. The air is filled with the lingering smell of incense and the tones of Gregorian chant – which can still be heard above the sound of the juke box downstairs and the siren of a passing police car.

As people enter the room they are presented with a sheet of paper on which is printed a scant order of service and a few prayers and readings for use throughout the evening. The theme is announced as 'God – Close Enough to Touch!' and for the following hour or so, through readings, meditation and the use of symbols, the gathered company explores aspects of divine immanence – the notion that God is present in the very substance of the material world. At a given point people are also encouraged to affirm God's presence in themselves, in their bodies and personalities, and to recognize that, though damaged and broken, the divine image is still reflected in who and what they are as individual people. An invitation is given to everyone to step forward, kneel in front of the triptych, and look into the broken mirrors, acknowledging the fragmented yet still visible image of God in their lives. Two or three at a time, people approach and peer, somewhat nervously to begin with, into the pieces of glass and, after a few moments' contemplation, light a candle, dip their finger in the oil and anoint themselves on the forehead as a symbolic way of accepting God's blessing on their lives. They then return to their places.

A young woman called Jenny, who wandered into the room at the start of the service by mistake, looking for a man she was supposed to meet in the pub, is so intrigued by the atmosphere and by what she sees going on that she forgets her date and asks if she can stay around. 'It's amazing,' Jenny commented later, 'I just couldn't leave. I'm not religious or anything, but this isn't like religion or church. It's more like a really relaxed chill-out room in a nightclub – but really spiritual as well.'

It is interesting that, despite the prayers, the clearly religious symbols and the nature of the whole event, Jenny likened her experience to a chill-out room rather than a church. Her sense was that something spiritual was going on, which drew her in, but which she didn't associate with church or religion.

Jenny's situation highlights the dilemma of the Church in Western societies today: lots of people are fascinated by spirituality, but few of them have any interest in going to church. A 'spirituality revolution' is going on while church attendance continues to decline.

According to the 'Soul of Britain' survey carried out by the BBC, the number of people in Britain who admitted to having had a spiritual experience increased during the 1990s by 59 per cent to a staggering 76 per cent. Yet only 7 per cent of those people attended church regularly. The results of the survey prompted researchers at the University of Nottingham to conclude that 'Something extraordinary appears to be happening to the spiritual life of Britain.'[1]

My own anecdotal observation as a parish priest working constantly with people who don't attend church is that the BBC survey is right, and although the poll was taken in 2000, the trend continues: I encounter people all the time who speak of spiritual experiences occurring in their lives.

Recently, I took the funeral of a two-week-old baby. After a harrowing service I spent most of the rest of the day in a pub with seventy or eighty relatives and friends of the family. When I returned home that evening I reflected on the forty or so conversations I must have had during the day. I realized that not a single person had asked me to justify my belief in God. How different that would have been twenty or thirty years ago. Instead, I was inundated with questions about things which, broadly speaking, come under the umbrella of 'spirituality'. People related many personal experiences, asking for my thoughts and reactions. We chatted about subjects ranging from yoga to astrology, from mediums to horror movies, from Feng Shui to spooky encounters with deceased relatives, from Zen meditation to Celtic spirituality, and much more besides. If there were atheists or full-on rationalists in the pub, they certainly didn't make their presence known.

So why are church attendances declining while interest in spirituality increases? If people are looking for the sense of belonging that I talked about in the previous chapter, why do they not look for it in the churches? Surely, churches are the obvious place to turn to? Well, apparently not. The fact is, most people do not think of churches as potential sources of spiritual nourishment. If this is going to change, churches need to discover what it means to become centres of living spirituality. When Jenny walked unintentionally into the pub service, she wasn't interested in religion or church or dogma, but she *was* fascinated by the spiritual energy she sensed. A huge gulf existed between the Spirited atmosphere she felt in that unglamorous upstairs room of the pub, and her perception of the Church as an irrelevant institution.

But it is Spirit that really counts. We can't re-enchant people with Church simply by replacing hymn books with computer images, or moving the services from a Victorian church to a city pub, or by substituting vestments with t-shirts and jeans. We need Spiritedness, not trendiness. Technology and informality will not save the Church. To do that, we need to reconnect with people's spirits, capture their imaginations, feed their hungry souls. It's about living the heart of Christian tradition in an authentically twenty-first-century fashion. Spirited authenticity is what we need.

Jenny was captivated by an unconventional approach to Christian spirituality in an unusual setting. But Stephanie was equally inspired when she came to a much more conventional confirmation service at St Luke's. She described the experience in an email to friends back home in New Zealand:

I went to church for the first time in England yesterday. I had a recommendation from someone in NZ for an Anglican church near my house. It was only ten minutes on the bus and it was excellent. An unassuming, intelligent minister and nice, normal-seeming people. I went again in the evening because they had a special confirmation service and we were asked to bring a bottle of wine to share afterwards – how could I resist?

The Bishop of London was speaking and doing the confirmations. He was a big man with a deep voice and English stage actor accent (lovely) and loads of presence. He wore his funny bishop's hat for some of it, and robes of gold and crimson and white that flowed off his shoulders to swim on the floor.

The church is full of stone arches, there was a medieval style triptych up the front, huge big candles, modern artwork on the walls. The service was quite straightforward and traditional – real hymns, a choir who sang some songs in Latin, which was beautiful – a mix of organ, piano and guitar – some African-style drumming.

The Bishop spoke warmly and richly; he used words like 'wrrrenched' (think rolled r's of posh accent) and 'astonishing' which sent shivers of delight through my soul. He was funny. When he was walking from the baptismal font to the front of the church he had to dip a fir tree frond in a big clear bowl of water and shake it over the congregation (symbolic of cleansing I suppose) and he did it with an undercurrent of frivolity that only added to the weight of spiritual meaning in what he was doing.

It was like he solemnly shook joy over us. We were allowed to laugh at something that was funny (having water thrown at you) and it was all the more beautiful and God-like. I felt that a real, thunderous and magical God was illuminated in that church. I went home singing and strengthened, although that sounds a bit weird.

Through the wonders of the internet, Stephanie's email did the rounds 'down under' and landed on my computer two days later!

What Stephanie experienced in that service was energizing Spirited ritual – a glorious mixture of numinosity, humour, humanity and animated tradition. Without these kinds of qualities, the Church's rites and rituals alienate rather than resonate. If religion cannot inspire people and empower them to process effectively the pleasures, pains and uncertainties of postmodern life, we might just as well close down.

The difference between ritual that energizes and empowers, and the sort of ritual that is lifeless ceremonial, is Spirit. A ritual without Spirit is like a river bed with no water. Indeed, the word 'ritual' actually derives from the Latin word *ritus*, meaning 'to flow, run, rush or stream'. A rite is a river; *rivus*, a rushing stream.[2] If the river has run dry, if our rites, rituals and liturgies lack Spirit, then the river ceases to exist. We may have a river bed – words, structures and formal activities – but we do not have a river. But if the river is flowing, ritual can have a massive, transforming effect on people's lives. The Church ceases to be an institution or a religious talk-shop and becomes a centre for spirituality.

Spirited ritual can do what words cannot do. It actually falls somewhere in the sphere of art: like music or a painting, or drama, it has an intuitive element; it draws on the right side of the brain, the side that processes reality in a non-rational, affective fashion. So it can reach the parts that words alone cannot. It can effectively and affectively resolve issues in people's lives; it can discharge healing energies in ways that reason alone fails to do.

The problem is that much church ritual fails to mediate life or Spirit. As the Catholic theologian Hans Küng observes, God has been obscured in our churches, and often by their actions, 'so that the only remaining possibility is to close one's eyes in order to turn inwards and find the all-encompassing, all-directing God in the secrecy of my inner self, to sense, feel, and experience him at the core of my being'. This is the Church's dilemma: worship and ritual frequently fail to connect people to the great inner quest; religion becomes either externalized in ceremonial or rationalized in dogma – either way, the numinous is lost in conventionality.

At its best, ritual can bring about a transformation. Every Sunday when the people of St Luke's leave their seats, process into the chancel, then stand shoulder-to-shoulder, slightly crushed around the altar and utter the words, 'Though we are many, we are one body, because we all share in one bread', a transformation takes place: a hodgepodge collection of friends and strangers, men and women, straight and gay, black and white, believers and doubters, stands before God as one, a community of grace. The task of this sacred ritual is not to say 'Abracadabra' and cause God to be present, but to reveal to people the God who is already present: to 'bind back' (*religio*) our lives and sufferings to a deeper, more profound presence. As David Tacey says, the function of the priest here is not to be a magician who goes 'Zap', but more of a 'poet or bard' pointing to the mysterious presence at the heart of the community.[3]

Yet sometimes the transforming energy of ritual is required in a more specific situation, and this is part of the Church's pastoral work too. After the painful breakdown of a marriage or partnership, for example, a rite of passage can be a powerful means of bringing healing, and enabling people to move on. Sometimes this might involve both parties, but often it is just one partner who seeks help. Let me give an example.

Susan struggled to feel confident to move into a new relationship, even six years after her divorce settlement. Pastoral counselling helped, but she needed something at an emotional level too, to release her from the guilt, pain and disappointment she experienced. My wife Pat suggested to her that a simple rite of passage might help. So we created a ritual with Susan, tailor-made to her particular perceived needs. The event took place during a dinner party with a dozen invited friends and family members. In the midst of the meal, Susan confessed her failure in the marriage – something she really felt the need to do. Then we all said to her, 'Susan, God forgives you. Forgive yourself.' A little later, she cut a symbolic ribbon at the door of the room and walked out, a liberated woman – who is now happily remarried with children.

I could give other examples with similar stories covering other situations in life. Even the more conventional offices of marriage, baptism and burial provide wonderful opportunities to collaborate with people in producing energizing ritual events that can transform people's lives and situations.

The only way forward for a dying tradition is to reconnect people to the source of that tradition. But it is a mistake to imagine that tradition has no part to play in the re-enchantment of Church. Rivers need water, but they also require a river bed. Spiritual energy detached from tradition is unsustainable. But as we have already seen, tradition is itself a conversation between past and present. When the conversation ceases, two things happen: first, tradition becomes traditionalism; it becomes rigid, inflexible, moribund and inhibitive of progress; and second, experience apart from a living tradition becomes superficial, lacking the depth, wisdom and rootedness of past encounters with the divine. A re-enchanted Church is a place of vigorous conversation between past and present, where religion cannot ossify into idolatry and bigotry, and where innovation cannot arrogantly dispense with the experience and wisdom of previous generations.

This is part of what it means for the Church to be an inclusive community: the past is recognized as an essential part of who we are in the present and who we need to be in the future. But being inclusive also means creating churches where anyone can find a place of loving acceptance – a place in which to belong. In a world of dislocation, fragmentation and estrangement, the Church is ideally placed to recreate community, offering somewhere where people can put down roots, where they can grow and flourish as people, as couples, as families, regardless of things like background, ethnicity, gender, education or sexuality.

The Church is by definition an inclusive community, because at its centre is the inclusive God whose love is manifest in the one who hung on a cross with arms outstretched. Church is not supposed to be a place of theological 'purity', or rigid conformity to certain beliefs and conventions, but a mishmash of believers, doubters, dissenters and malcontents, each of whom is grappling in his or her own way towards the mystery that is God. The Church is a place of refuge and hope, a place of prayer and laughter, a place of dreams and fresh imagining, a place of birth and rebirth, a place of welcome and acceptance, a place of thought and theology, a place of weddings and funerals, a place where proud mums and dads bring tiny people to offer them to God, a place of parties, a place of bread and wine shared, a place of affirmation, a place of new beginnings, a place of freedom and generosity, a place of friendship, support and healing, a place of creativity, a place of reconciliation, a place of faith and doubt, a place where people can belong without necessarily knowing how or what to believe.

Notes

1 David Tacey, *The Spirituality Revolution: the Emergence of Contemporary Spirituality*, Hove: Brunner-Routledge, 2004, p. 15.
2 Tacey, *The Spirituality Revolution*, p. 23.
3 Tacey, *The Spirituality Revolution*, p. 169.

13

Synergizing the Soul

Making sense of prayer

'I don't believe in an interventionist God!' is the opening line
of Nick Cave's wonderful love song, 'Into my Arms'. It surely
stands as the most blatantly theological statement in the history of rock music, plunging the listener headlong into theology's most profound questions: What is God like? How does
God relate to the universe? And what can we expect when we
pray?

I suspect that all of us – including Nick Cave – want God to
be an interventionist God at times: when we desperately crave
something that we can't have, when we long to see a loved
one healed of an incurable disease, or when we would happily
see some God-awful tyrant zapped almightily from on high!
And there are plenty of Christians who think that, fundamentally, this is how prayer works: like ordering something on
the internet – you open your 'account' with God, make your
request known through prayer, and then sit back and wait for
the 'goods' to arrive. Prayer is the magic solution to all of life's
problems, however great or small.

Yet prayer cannot be that straightforward. For example, if
God really does intervene in human affairs, why is it done in
such a spasmodic and weirdly selective fashion? What criteria
does God use in deciding when and where to intervene? Why
would the Almighty find a parking spot for a person simply
because they are late for an appointment, or why heal some
trivial condition like warts, or grant a request for a sunny day
tomorrow because it's the church barbecue? Surely divine time
and energy would be better spent averting a tsunami, or pro-

viding food for the starving, or helping a small child escape torture and abuse in the sex industry?

The idea of divine intervention in response to prayer is surely an absurdity. Well, yes – except I confess that I personally pray for things to happen all the time. Not that, for one moment, I imagine prayer working in some crude cause-and-effect fashion; yet I can't get rid of the gut feeling that it does matter whether or not we pray for people and situations.

So, intellectually and theologically, I have real problems with the idea of divine intervention, but in practical terms, I seem to ask God to do things all the time. Actually, Nick Cave's song reflects some of this ambivalence too: 'I don't believe in an interventionist God ... But if I did I would kneel down and ask him ...' The rest of the song meanders around this paradox.

The problem centres on the question of what we mean by 'intervention'. The term assumes a transcendent God 'out there' somewhere else, 'up in heaven' deciding on some basis or other whether or not to 'intervene' in particular human situations. This is not how I see God. As I explained earlier in the book, my understanding of God's relationship with the world is encapsulated in the notion of panentheism – the belief that God is *in* all things and all things are *in* God. I should emphasize once more that this is entirely different from pantheism, which says that God *is* everything and everything *is* God. Panentheism seeks to maintain a tension between divine transcendence and divine immanence. In declaring God to be transcendent we are saying that God is 'more' than the universe. By saying that God is immanent we are declaring that God is present in the universe – as the cosmic Spirit, the life-force in everything.

When we think of God as the Spirit of the cosmos, or as the 'encompassing Spirit' as Marcus Borg puts it, we find ourselves replacing 'divine intervention' with 'divine intention' or 'divine interaction' with the world.[1] From this perspective we neither see God as some great conductor of human affairs pushing buttons and throwing switches, nor as a disengaged deity impervious to human affairs and the world's suffering. Instead, we understand God to be radically involved, interconnected and interactive with life on planet earth, and indeed with the universe as a whole.

So, can God 'make things happen' as a result of prayer? I'm not sure that is the right question. As Walter Wink puts it: 'When we pray, we are not sending a letter to a celestial White House, where it is sorted among piles of others. We are engaged, rather, in an act of co-creation, in which one little sector of the universe rises up and becomes translucent, incandescent, a vibratory centre of power that radiates the power of the universe.'[2]

The danger lies in trying to say too much at this point, of trying to understand the mysterious mechanism behind God's interaction with the world. However, the way I see it is like this: I understand that the divine Spirit works in and with the world as it is in order to bring it towards what it can be.[3] This is what Paul is getting at with his wonderful description of the whole creation groaning with labour pains, and us groaning along with it, in anticipation of what the world and we can be, the new creation (Rom. 8.19–25). In the same passage Paul goes on to talk about the Spirit praying within us with a deep sighing too deep for words to utter. This sighing is the profound longing of the cosmos – felt within us too – for healing and fulfilment in the divine purpose.

So yes, I do pray – not for divine intervention, but in order that my spirit – and my entire life – may become synergized with God's Spirit, the life-force of the universe, in bringing to fruition God's will on earth. Does this mean that Uncle Billy's gout will get better when I pray about it? I'm not sure, but I'll carry on praying anyway, not least because it focuses my concern for Uncle Billy, and reminds me to go and see him more often.

We mostly think of prayer in terms of words: words of request or petition, words of thankfulness, words of intercession for others, words of worship or adoration. But prayer is about far more than words; and the deepest prayers cannot be put into words. Sometimes prayer is quiet contemplation, sometimes it is a gesture such as lighting a candle or kneeling, sometimes it is a stroll in the country or a walk down a busy street, sometimes it is an act of kindness, or a kiss, or a meal lovingly cooked, or a protest against injustice, or a hearty burst of laughter. Prayer is the heart engaging with life, engaging with the Spirit of life, engaging with God. In this sense, prayer doesn't have to do with religion, nor does it have to find expression in religious terms. I agree with Frederick Buechner: everyone prays, whether he or she thinks of it as praying or not:

> The odd silence you fall into when something very beautiful is happening or something very good or very bad. The ah-h-h-h! that sometimes floats up out of you as out of a Fourth of July crowd when the sky-rocket bursts over the water. The stammer of pain at somebody else's pain. The stammer of joy at somebody else's joy. Whatever sounds you use for sighing with over your own life. These are all prayers in their own way. These are all spoken not just to yourself but to something even more familiar than yourself and even more strange than the world.[4]

Whether formal and liturgical, or extempore, whether carefully planned, or impromptu; whether expressed through choral evensong, a Hindu mantra, a 'Hari Krishna' chant, the turning of a Tibetan Buddhist prayer wheel, the repetitious invoking of the name of Allah, a Kvitel offered at the Wailing Wall, or the mumbling of the rosary while beads are fingered – prayer is the trembling expression of the soul's yearning. Even the profane blurting of 'God Almighty!' can be truly a prayer.

As Paul indicates, the most profound expressions of prayer – indeed the very basis of all prayer and of religion itself – is the deep sighing of God's Spirit within that cannot be put into words. I think that this is what Nick Cave is referring to in an insightful lecture entitled, 'The Secret Life of the Love Song'.[5] He talks about a deep inner longing as the source of all real art. The Portuguese have a word for it, Cave says, *saudade* (sow-dah-je), which translates as an inexplicable sense of longing, a yearning of the soul. This almost primal yearning can never be properly articulated, only hinted at or referred to obliquely; it can only be felt, 'and all we know of it is that it is what we are looking for'. As Elizabeth Bassett observes, this yearning 'can become misdirected into channels which lead to drugs or drink or other excesses for excitement to assuage the longing when it has not been recognized for what it is'. In some way or other, the whole of life is concerned with this yearning, which 'carries us on into death and beyond when we dare to hope that we shall come face to face with the source of all our longing'.[6]

Prayer is about making the connection with the Spirit of life, *ruach*, the life-force in all created beings. Whether through stammering words, images, meditation or silence, prayer is making that connection. It's about waking up: waking up to ourselves, waking up to other people and to situations around us, waking up to God. Waking up to new possibilities, and then working towards their fulfilment.

Buddhists talk about the process of spiritually waking up as 'mindfulness'. Mindfulness is the conscious decision to be present right where we are. It is a deliberate choosing to be aware of the people and things around us. It involves cultivating a habit of attentiveness. Noticing the various colours of the goldfinch feeding in the garden, listening to the other person without letting our mind wander or hastily formulating a reply, listening to our own selves without judgement or criticism.

Children are much better than adults at mindful praying. Just go for a walk with a child. Every stone or leaf or insect is an item of beauty and fascination. Every moment is lived. But adults find this really hard, because it involves letting go of the priorities and 'necessities' that drive us on from one situation to the next without making any real connections. Yet, to be mindful, to indwell the moment, to be attentive to some detail of creation is not only to become more authentically human, but also to engage in an act of true praise to God.

Taking a short time each day to make that connection, to pray and be mindful, will be life changing, because we are plugging into the life-force of the universe, the Spirit of God.

But it is not just beauty to which prayer can make us more attentive, we can also become more aware of pain and suffering in the world. Jürgen Moltmann writes:

In prayer we wake up to the world as it is spread out before God in all its heights and depths. We perceive the sighing of creation, and hear the cries of the created victims that have fallen dumb. We also hear the song of praise of the blossoming spring, and feel the divine love for everything that lives. So prayer to God awakens all our senses and alerts our minds and spirits. The person who prays, lives more attentively.[7]

When asked what he thought was the most important question facing humanity, Albert Einstein replied, 'I think the most important question facing humanity is, "Is the universe a friendly place?"' Einstein wasn't simply posing a theological conundrum. He understood that the way we answer that question would have profound implications for the way we live and develop as a global community. But it also has a significant bearing on the way we comprehend the meaning and purpose of prayer. The basis of all prayer is the belief that the universe is indeed a friendly place; that we are not alone, that there exists at the heart of the cosmos a benevolent Being, whom we identify as God. Our trembling words are uttered into the darkness because we are convinced that someone is there, someone listens, someone cares; because we are convinced that our frail lives and concerns actually matter. To pray is to affirm that there is someone: an identifiable knowable, reachable You, who is the Spirit of the cosmos, the ground and source of all life.

There is a wonderful old rabbinic prayer reiterated by the Jewish philosopher Martin Buber that says:

Where I wander – You!
Where I ponder – You!
Only You, You again, always You!
You! You! You!

When I am gladdened – You!
When I am saddened – You!
Only You, You again, always You!
You! You! You!
Sky is You! Earth is You!
You above! You below!
In every trend, at every end,
Only You, You again, always You!
You! You! You![8]

To recognize and reach out to this You is to transform the inner landscape of one's being; it is to reconfigure the context of one's life from a monologue to a dialogue. We will never quite feel alone again. Someone is there. Someone hears our inmost thoughts. Someone reads our truest intentions. Someone comprehends our deepest longings – and loves us unconditionally.

Prayer is about a way of being in the presence of the divine Other. It is the realization that, as my friend Martin Wroe writes:

God is
where you are
when you're at the end of yourself.
God is
who you are with
when you are with no one at all.
God is
that feeling you have
when you're not sure your feelings can be trusted.
God is
underneath everything,
above,
not beyond,
and sometimes
just side by side,
leaning across,
waiting for an invite.[9]

Notes

1 Marcus Borg, *The Heart of Christianity: How We Can Be Passionate Believers Today*, New York: HarperCollins, 2003, p. 66f.

2 Walter Wink, *The Powers That Be: Theology for a New Millennium*, New York: Doubleday, 1998, p. 186f.

3 Marjorie Hewitt Suchocki, *In God's Presence: Theological Reflections on Prayer*, St Louis: Chalice Press, 1996, p. 31.

4 Frederick Buechner, *Beyond Words*, New York: HarperCollins, 2004, p. 320.

5 'The Secret Life of the Love Song' by Nick Cave is available as a CD on the Mute label. A transcript can be found at <http://everything2.com/index.pl?node_id=800055>.

6 Elizabeth Bassett, *The Bridge is Love*, London: Darton, Longman & Todd, 1981, p. 31.

7 Jürgen Moltmann, *In the End – the Beginning*, London: SCM Press, 2003, p. 83.

8 Martin Buber, *Tales of the Hasidim*, Milan: Milan Press, 1979, p. 256.

9 Martin Wroe, *The Sky's Window*, London: The WroeYourBoat Publishing, 2006, p. 73.

14

This is My Truth, Tell Me Yours

Is God bigger than Christianity?

A friend of mine went on a trip to the Balkans some years ago
to help build new homes. The venture was part of a Christian
charitable project to foster social regeneration after the war
in that region in the early 1990s. As the convoy approached
a border crossing, the flow of traffic was held up for a couple
of hours. Looking out of the vehicle in the mid-afternoon, my
friend and his companions witnessed the impressive sight of
hundreds of Muslims leaving their cars to kneel on the grass
at the side of the road for afternoon prayers. Struck by their
devotion to this spiritual practice, my friend commented on
what a wonderful sight it was. One of his fellow travellers replied, nonchalantly, 'Yes. It's a shame they're all going to hell,
isn't it?'

I grew up in a church where that kind of outlook was ubi-
quitous – though I don't think it would have been expressed in
such a callous manner. I remember as a child being unable to
sleep after hearing a 'gospel' message preached which talked
about how the people of other religions would go to hell if they
failed to accept Christ as their Saviour. It didn't seem fair to
me. Why was I lucky enough to be born in a Christian country
with Christian parents? Would God really reject millions of
people just because they were born in the 'wrong' country?
Would I go to hell if I had been born there and not accepted
Jesus? I couldn't get my head around it all.

And the questions didn't leave me when I grew up. As a
preacher and church leader, I taught that salvation was in
Christ alone, yet persistent doubts loitered in the recesses of

my mind. I suppose I managed to file them away, with ump-teen other nasty niggling questions, in a mental folder labelled 'Too hard to sort out right now'!

That file was flung wide open one day in the middle of a planning meeting for a large Christian event which I was to speak at. I was asked to lead a seminar with two other speak-ers in which we would each take twenty minutes to talk about the errors either of Islam, Hinduism or Buddhism. I was as-signed Buddhism.

'But I don't really know anything about Buddhism', I ob-jected. 'Oh don't worry, it's all in the notes', was the reply. But the notes didn't help. In fact they made my blood pressure rocket so high I nearly had a heart attack on the spot! 'This is a hatchet job!', I said. 'If a non-Christian wrote something like this about Christianity we would go ballistic, and rightly so.' Needless to say, this did not go down too well – as also my sug-gestion that we should get some people of other faiths to the event to have a real debate. By the end of the meeting it was felt that I probably wasn't the best person to address the subject. What a relief! Yet, looking back, I am thankful for that meet-ing, because it proved to be a turning point in my attitude to-wards other faiths; I finally pulled the question out of the 'Too hard to sort out right now' file and started to face up to it.

The problem with the exclusivist approach to religion (the assumption that we and only we have the truth) is that it pur-ports to know too much. It also frequently results in smug and distinctly un-Christian attitudes. The interesting thing is that the deconstruction of religious certainty actually exists in the Bible itself. Walter Brueggemann offers a marvellously enlight-ening example of this in an essay on the prophetic message of Amos to Israel in the eighth century BC, which I will draw on in the following thoughts.[1]

One way to summarize Amos' message to Israel would be: 'God has had it up to here with your empty religion!' 'God hates your religious feasts,' Amos says, 'your ceremonies, your solemn assemblies, your burnt offerings, your noisy songs and your twanging harps' (Amos 5.21–24). God wanted action, not religion from Israel: justice for the poor, a fair deal for the needy, an end to corruption and abuse. 'Let justice roll down like waters,' Amos said, 'and righteousness like an ever flowing stream' (5.24).

But Amos went further, telling them that their profoundly held belief that they were God's special people was flawed. The problem lay in what Brueggemann refers to as Israel's 'only-ness'. As well as believing that Yahweh was the *only* true God, they also believed that Israel was Yahweh's *only* true people. They became 'self-satisfied' and 'self-congratulatory' about their religion, their ethics and their worship; their 'orthodoxy' became 'a warrant for self-indulgence'.[2]

Brueggemann's essay focuses mainly on just one verse, Amos 9.7, where God poses two deceptively subversive questions to Israel:

Are you not like the Ethiopians to me, O people of Israel? says the Lord. Did I not bring Israel up from the land of Egypt, and the Philistines from Caphtor and the Arameans from Kir?

Israel makes no reply in the text, though there can be little doubt what they would have wanted to say: a categorical 'No!' on both counts. No, the Ethiopians are not like us – no one is like us. And no, you did not deliver the Philistines and the Arameans (Israel's two traditional enemies) in the way you delivered Israel from Egypt! But the implication of the question is very clear: God does indeed have a redemptive history with other peoples, not unlike his history with Israel. God has many 'client peoples' to whom he attends in powerful, liberating ways. There can be, therefore, Brueggemann says, 'no single "salvation history", no fixed line of "God's mighty deeds", for such "mighty deeds" happen in many places, many of which are beyond the purview of Israel's orthodoxy'.[3] God is at work in other ways, in other histories, in order to effect other liberations.[4] God will not be 'contained in or domesticated by Israel's exclusivist ideology'.[5]

Brueggemann goes on to point out that God's liberating intervention to these other peoples did not lead to their conversion to Yahwism; it did not require them to speak Hebrew, or to submerge their histories as subsets of Israel's history. Indeed, it is perfectly reasonable to assume, he says, that the exodus God came to be known to the Philistines and the Syrians, if at all, in Philistine and Syrian modes. God is 'enormously pliable and supple as a participant in the histories of many peoples'.[6]

Brueggemann does not extrapolate from his exposition of Amos 9.7 on present-day inter-faith relations. Yet the 'radical pluralism', which he sees Amos as introducing into the character of Yahweh,[7] should give great pause for thought as we contemplate the attitude of Christian theology towards other religious communities. Surely, we can never presume that we and we alone know the truth, or presume to be party to precisely how, when and where God chooses to work or to be revealed.

How, then, should we look upon other religions? Are we supposed to try to convert them all to Christianity, or can we accept that perhaps God is leading them by a different route? Is God bigger than Christianity? The key issue for those of us who are receptive to the prospect of God working or being revealed within other faith communities is how to sustain this stance while also maintaining the integrity of our own faith – and in particular, the testimony that in Christ we find the definitive focus of God's acting and presence in the world.

Before coming to that, let's step back and identify the recognized main approaches to religious theory. Following the work of John Hick (theologian and philosopher of religion) in particular, these tend to fall into three categories.[8] The first is called the *exclusivist* view, which asserts that there is no truth or genuine relation to God to be found outside the Christian faith. The opposite extreme of this is the *pluralist* view, which recognizes truth everywhere in all the faith traditions; different religions simply represent different ways of saying the same thing. The *inclusivist* view that lies somewhere between the other two allows for the possibility that genuine knowledge and experience of God may exist in other traditions, but most-ly holds that Christianity represents the normative and ulti-mate revelation of God.

Much of my earlier Christian life was orientated around the exclusivist model, which I clearly now reject as being too con-fident and verbose in its approach to God, and too dismissive of the possibility of God being revealed in other ways through people of other faiths, or none. However, I find the plural-ist view – a thoroughgoing relativism – equally unsatisfactory, because this says too little of any consequence about God. It does well at identifying the commonalities between the reli-gions, but fails to encompass their differences, some of which are contradictory. Everything cannot be equally true, so we need some basis to decide what we accept and what we reject. The inclusivist view appears to be the best option of the three; however, I can't accept the patronizing strategy of being inclus-ive by transforming members of other faith communities into 'anonymous Christians', as Karl Rahner famously puts it.[9]

I am convinced that it is possible to maintain fully the in-tegrity of one's own faith while also accepting the prospect of God being revealed within other faith communities. But I pre-fer to adopt the rather straightforward policy of 'openness *and* commitment', a phrase introduced by John Macquarrie.[10] His argument is that commitment and openness are required of us, not least because of our limitations as human beings: since we cannot possibly know everything, we need to remain open to the insights and experiences of others, and since we cannot be committed to everything, we need to commit to a particular way or tradition. It is perfectly possible, in his view, to take the claims of the Christian tradition as definitive without absolu-tizing them in a way that dismisses the insights and wisdom of other traditions.

In trying to retain the necessary tension between openness and commitment, it is helpful to be reminded that christological affirmations are statements about Jesus, not about people of various other faiths. As theologian David Lochhead points out, the confessional claim that God is revealed definitively

in Jesus Christ carries no necessary implication that members
of other faith communities lie beyond the providence of God.
In order to arrive at that conclusion, some additional premise
such as 'Human salvation is dependent on *explicit* faith in
Jesus Christ', would be required. 'This qualification, however,
is not the necessary consequence of a high Christology. It is
a distinct and additional theological premise in conservative
evangelical missiology.'[11]

Once again, it is important to bear in mind the lesson from
Amos, where Israel's mistake was not to affirm that they were
God's chosen people, but to imagine that *they alone* were
God's chosen people. It is vital not to say more than we can
say, or need to say; or to claim more than we can legitimately
claim.

Hans Küng develops the notion of 'commitment and openness' by talking about 'dialogue and steadfastness'.[12] Steadfastness is very similar to commitment; it is about self-assertion,
not giving in, holding firm, having courage and resolution.
But dialogue is expressing something much more positive and
proactive than openness. Openness is a virtuous but possibly
passive quality. Dialogue makes openness work for a living;
it puts it into action. Dialogue is based on the conviction that
there is something to dialogue about: ideas, insights and experiences to be gained as well as shared. Far from being just passively open, dialogue clears the ground for creative interaction,
for a new energy to surface. It is an activity that can occur
between people who have a standpoint – a truth to hold fast
to – yet who respect the standpoints of others, and who also
acknowledge that there are always new things to learn.

Küng poses the question: 'If one believes in Christ as the
way, the truth and the life, can one then also accept that there
are other ways, other truths, that there is other life from transcendence? The Torah? The Qur'an? The Eightfold Path of the
Buddha? So can openness and truth, plurality and identity,
capacity for dialogue and steadfastness, be combined in inter-
religious dialogue?' In other words, is there a theologically
responsible way that allows Christians to accept the truth of

other religions without giving up the truth of their own faith convictions and thus their own identity? Küng lays out his own criteria for what he calls 'a critically ecumenical standpoint'.

- No indifferentism for which everything is of equal value, but more indifference over alleged orthodoxy which makes itself the criterion for human salvation or damnation and seeks to impose its claim to truth by means of power and compulsion.
- No relativism for which there is no Absolute, but rather more sense of relativity in all that human beings make absolute and that prevents a productive co-existence of the various religions, and of relationality, which makes it possible to see every religion in its web of relationships.
- No syncretism, where everything possible and impossible is mixed together and fused, but more will for synthesis, for slow growing together in the face of all confessional and religious oppositions and antagonisms which still cost blood and tears every day, so that peace can prevail between religions instead of war and strife.[13]

Building on a foundation of 'steadfastness and dialogue', Küng was a key player in the production of a statement of a 'global ethic' – a declaration of intent for religious communities to work together in pursuing common goals for the good of all. The outcome of this declaration, presented to the Parliament of the World's Religions in 1993, included four essential affirmations for a global ethic:

1 Commitment to a culture of non-violence and respect for life.
2 Commitment to a culture of solidarity and a just economic order.
3 Commitment to a culture of tolerance and a life of truthfulness.
4 Commitment to a culture of equal rights and partnership between men and women.[14]

More than 200 leaders from over forty different religious traditions and spiritual communities signed the declaration, the full text of which can be found on the website of the Global Ethic Foundation.[15] Thousands more have signed it since. The events following 9/11 add massive poignancy to the declaration, and to Küng's dictum: 'No peace among nations without peace among religions.' In a world torn apart by war, violence and terrorism, much of which cannot be disentangled from religion and religious conflicts, we desperately need people of good faith across the world's religions to work together with a common global ethic for just and peaceful settlements in regions of strife and conflict.

We no longer live in a world where the different faith communities are separated by thousands of miles on different continents. We live in a global community, and an increasingly pluralist society. The prospect of rising levels of competition between the world's religions, and between Christianity and Islam in particular, casts an ominous shadow over the future in the twenty-first century. It would be much better, writes John Taylor, to think of entering a period of mutual testimony, in which the witnesses will not always agree, but where each will contribute their conviction and try to grasp the inwardness of what the other is saying. 'And the Christian contribution is that God is Christlike.'[16]

Notes

1 Walter Brueggemann, '"Exodus" in the Plural (Amos 9:7)', in Walter Brueggemann and George W. Stroup (eds), *Many Voices, One God*, Louisville: Westminster John Knox Press, 1998.

2 Brueggemann, '"Exodus"', p. 19.

3 Brueggemann, '"Exodus"', p. 22.

4 Brueggemann, '"Exodus"', p. 25.

5 Brueggemann, '"Exodus"', p. 22.

6 Brueggemann, '"Exodus"', p. 25f.

7 Brueggemann, '"Exodus"', p. 20.

8 See, for example, John Hick, *God Has Many Names: Britain's New Religious Pluralism*, London: Macmillan, 1980.

9 Karl Rahner, *Theological Investigations*, Vol. 16, translated by David Morland, London: Darton, Longman & Todd, 1979, p. 18.

10 John Macquarrie, *Theology, Church and Ministry*, London: SCM Press, 1986, p. 148.

11 This is an argument developed in David Lochhead, *The Dialogical Imperative*, London: SCM Press, 1988, p. 90ff.

12 Hans Küng, *Global Responsibility: In search of a New World Ethic*, London: SCM Press, 1991, p. 94ff.

13 Küng, *Global Responsibility*, p. 96f.

14 Hans Küng and Karl-Josef Kuschel (eds), *A Global Ethic: the Declaration of the Parliament of the World's Religions*, London: SCM Press, 1993.

15 The full text of the Global Ethic declaration can be found in *A Global Ethic: The Declaration of the Parliament of the World's Religions*, or at the website of the Global Ethic Foundation, <www.weltethos.org/dat-english/03-declaration.htm>.

16 John Taylor, 'The Future of Christianity', in John McManners (ed.), *The Oxford Illustrated History of Christianity*, Oxford: Oxford University Press, 1992, p. 652.

15

Mission Statement

Christianity in an emerging culture

One could be forgiven nowadays for imagining that some management guru like Stephen Covey invented the word 'mission'. His inspiring international bestseller, *The Seven Habits of Highly Effective People*, is just one of a plethora of management manuals that extol the benefits to organizations, families and individuals of developing a 'mission statement' – a stated 'creed' or 'philosophy' that helps people to identify who they are, who they wish to be, what they want to achieve, and what are the values and principles that will undergird their being and doing.[1]

The English word 'mission' was introduced by the Jesuits in the late sixteenth century – long before the invention of management seminars and personal coaching sessions! But the idea of mission (of being 'sent') in the Christian context goes back to the so-called 'great commission', where Christ sends his disciples to spread the gospel throughout the world.

Nowadays, Christian mission is a gigantic multi-billion-pound enterprise, devoted to evangelism, church planting, aid projects, campaigns for peace and social justice, and much more. Mission is a highly multifaceted endeavour, some aspects of which I personally find exciting and inspiring, while other parts leave me cold. Some expressions of present-day mission contribute to making the world a better, more peaceful, more just place in which to live, while others contribute to making it more divided and dangerous.

In this chapter I would like to outline my own 'mission statement': to identify what I think really matters about Christian mission in the emerging world of the twenty-first century. In some ways this may not differ from what one might say about mission in any other century, yet in other ways it is completely different. Mission is not a set of activities that can be learned from a manual or copied from previous generations; mission is the act of interpreting and expressing God's loving presence in the world in ways that resonate with or are relevant to a particular cultural and historical context with its peculiar needs and opportunities.

So for me, mission is not about trying to get people 'saved', or trying to get them to join the Church, or even about trying to get them to convert to Christianity. Mission is about making God's liberating love and peace and justice a flesh-and-blood reality in ways that can potentially transform people's lives, or potentially transform a neighbourhood, or potentially transform the world.

However, a huge problem exists for Christian mission today: the negative perceptions that people in the Western world have about the Church and Christianity. I know this from personal experience, working as a parish priest in the wider community: a large proportion of my time and energy is focused on overcoming these perceptions, and on re-forming and re-framing people's understanding of the Christian faith.

In his enlightening and challenging book, *The Spirituality Revolution: The Emergence of Contemporary Spirituality*, David Tacey identifies some of these negative perceptions of religion, which he says are typical of many people today:

- Religion is patriarchal and masculinist. It oppresses women, and excludes the feminine dimension of the divine.
- Religion is based on a pre-modern cosmology, with an externalist and interventionist God inhabiting a distant metaphysical space.
- Religion is based on a conception of spirit that is supernatural – an outside agency that works miracles – which seems wholly implausible and unattractive to modern understanding.

- Religion does not have enough to say about the experience of the sacred in creation. It is anthropocentric and does not teach us to live harmoniously with nature.
- Religion focuses on moral perfection instead of 'wholeness'.
- Religion is dualistic and instructs the spirit to triumph over the body and bodily desires. By contrast, the new spirituality seeks to bring spirit and body, sacredness and sexuality, together in a redemptive experience of the totality and mystery of life.
- Religion is hierarchical and elitist. Its investment of spiritual authority in clerical authority figures is outdated and distrusted. It rules from above and excludes the voice of the people and democratic understanding.
- Religion is dogmatic and external to our lives. It imposes laws and rules upon us, without enquiring into the nature of the self that it is seeking to transform. It does not offer a psychology or pathway for personal transformation, but simply demands conformity to devotional practices.
- Religion imposes the 'big story' of theology upon our experience, without exploring the 'little stories' of our individual biographies, which might give theology a foothold in our lives. Religion is rejected not because a person does not believe, but because he or she is not believed. If religion could incorporate the spirituality of individuals, it might be renewed within itself, and individuals would feel included, their experience valued.
- Religion does not provide enough challenge to society – to business, government and commercial enterprise – but simply reinforces and supports its basic values and, as such, it cannot represent the life of the spirit.[2]

I find it interesting that the classic apologetic issues concerning things like the tenability of belief in God in a scientific age are hardly represented in this list. The issue today does not seem to be whether or not God might exist, but rather what kind of God people can believe in. However, the real challenge to be faced from Tacey's list of perceptions is how to convince people that Christianity offers a life-affirming spirituality. My own experience of associating with and listening to non-churchgoers bears out Tacey's observation: many people today are spiritually hungry and receptive, yet they seldom imagine that Christianity – much less, the Church – may have something to contribute to satisfying that hunger. In their minds, Church and Christianity are generally associated with beliefs and dogma, with what they see as redundant moral standards, with conservative attitudes and conformist behaviour, but not with life-affirming spirituality.

If people in the West are going to be attracted back to Christianity as a way of channelling and expressing their spiritual instincts, this situation must be reversed. Fundamentally, we need to recover the heart and energy of the *missio dei*, the mission of God, which has everything to do with spreading a life-affirming spirituality, and nothing to do with setting up or sustaining mere religion. The mission of God, Jürgen Moltmann asserts, is 'nothing less than the sending of the Holy Spirit from the Father through the Son into this world, so that this world should not perish but live ... The sending of the Holy Spirit is the revelation of God's indestructible affirmation of life and his marvellous joy in life.'[3]

The mission of God was not to invent Christianity but to spread life. We must find ways, therefore, that lead 'from religion to the kingdom of God, from the church to the world, from concern about our own selves to hope for the whole'.[4]

So what should the priorities be for Christian mission in the emerging world of the twenty-first century?

1. Christian mission in the twenty-first century requires a kingdom orientation, rather than a church orientation

Don Cupitt wonderfully writes: 'What Jesus preached was "the kingdom"; what he got was the church!'

It is very clear that the thing that preoccupied Jesus constantly was the kingdom of God. We could even say it was his obsession. But what is the kingdom? For many people, this is a phrase that may evoke images of patriarchy, authoritarianism and hierarchy. It may be useful to point out straight away that in Aramaic (the language Jesus spoke) the word *malkuta*, translated 'kingdom', is feminine gendered, as is *basileia*, the Greek equivalent. But irrespective of this, it is very clear from the way that Jesus proclaimed God's kingdom that he did not have in mind a hierarchical or authoritarian system.

'Kingdom' also does not denote a territory or geographic location, but the reigning of divine love. It represents a vision of how things in the world are supposed to be. John Dominic Crossan, the Irish-American religious scholar, says that, 'the phrase evokes an ideal vision of political and religious power, of how this world here below would be if God, not Caesar, sat on the imperial throne'.[5]

Yet the term 'kingdom of God' is inescapably political. Of course it is. 'Jesus could have spoken of the "family" of God or the "community" of God, but he chose to speak of the "kingdom" of God',[6] a distinctly political designation. By political, I am not suggesting that it is tied to particular political systems, whether of the right or the left, but that it is about transforming the human situation at all levels. Jesus' vision of God's kingdom is encapsulated in the simple yet profound line of the Lord's Prayer: 'your kingdom come, your will be done, on earth as it is in heaven'. Dominic Crossan loves to say: 'Heaven is in great shape; earth is where the problem is.'[7]

The kingdom of God is a 'companionship of empowerment', Crossan concludes.[8] This is in response to his own rhetorical question: does the kingdom of God denote a realm of domination or of empowerment? It was the very programme of empowerment that Jesus followed that meant it couldn't be destroyed by executing him.[9] Throughout his life and ministry, Jesus constantly empowered people: people whose lives were dominated by sickness, prejudice, social discrimination, injustice, self-hatred and rejection. Relentlessly, people's lives were reordered and redefined by the transforming, empowering love of God manifest in Christ. In contrast to the 'barbarism of death',[10] Jesus introduced a culture of life, hope and liberation.

These are the key elements in kingdom-orientated mission: empowerment, justice, liberation, hope, healing and new life.

One very inspiring grass-roots example of kingdom-orientated mission can be found in the work of Umthombo, an initiative to help street kids in Durban, South Africa. Thousands of orphans and vulnerable children live on South Africa's streets. Abandoned, often raped, abused, infected with HIV/AIDS and driven to crime and prostitution, street kids are considered a nuisance, a threat and an embarrassment to the authorities. Umthombo is a unique project in that it is predominantly run and staffed by former street children themselves, and is a voice for street children across the region. Umthombo is indeed replacing the barbarism of death with a culture of life. It brings healing, dignity and self-worth to the neglected, downtrodden and disempowered fringes of human society. But it is also a companionship of empowerment, creating a new community of solidarity, and educating young people to think politically and theologically about their situation and to be organized in pursuing social justice for themselves and others.

Umthombo is not an evangelistic organization in the narrow sense of the term; it doesn't exist to 'preach Jesus' or plant new churches, but rather to spread life, hope and liberation through empowerment, through acts of love and social justice, through being an agent of hope and transformation both of individual lives and of an entire social circumstance. This is kingdom-orientated rather than church-orientated mission.

Sadly, a lot of mission has lost (or never discovered) this point of reference. The problem arises from confusion between the Church and the kingdom. The mission of God is to establish the kingdom in the world, and the Church is an agent or servant of that mission. 'There is church because there is mission, not vice versa.'[11] When the Church sees itself as the object of God's mission, it easily becomes triumphalist, imagining that the flourishing of the Church automatically equates with the flourishing of the kingdom of God. But this is not necessarily the case.

One feature that has historically preserved the Church of

England from confusing the Church with the kingdom is the notion of the parish, by which we recognize that the family of the Church is part of the larger family of the parish community. My job, therefore, is not only to serve as the chaplain or pastor of the congregation who meet regularly at St Luke's, but also to serve as a priest to the parish. And there are many people who seldom, if ever, appear in church services who consider me to be their spiritual guide. There is something healthy about this. It reminds us that the kingdom of God is bigger than the church congregation; that God is at work in the lives of people who don't attend church regularly, in the lives of people of other faiths and none.

Traces of God's kingdom can be recognized wherever love is shared, where life is truly lived and justice is sought, where freedom is experienced, and fear is overcome. Indeed, wherever God's healing, reconciling, inclusive will is enacted on earth as it is in heaven, God's reign is present. There are glimpses and echoes of this all over the place – in loving families, in all kinds of sacrificial acts, in the campaign Make Poverty History, in Red Nose Day, in a young man helping an elderly woman onto the bus, in simple acts of kindness shown to friends and strangers alike, in attempts to resolve conflicts and bring wars to an end, in efforts to preserve the world for future generations, in adding beauty to people's lives through art and music, in forgiveness when it's not deserved, in the daily fulfilment of jobs and callings that make people's lives happier and more fulfilled. These and so many other things contribute in some way to answering the prayer, 'Your kingdom come; your will be done, on earth as it is in heaven.'

I love John Henson's radical paraphrase of Philippians 4.8: 'There are plenty of good things in this world for you to appreciate and enjoy. There are many forms of truth, many causes that deserve support, campaigns for justice, societies with a good name, projects which benefit the community. These are things you ought to be interested in.'[12]

From a kingdom-orientated perspective we can say that the division in the world is not between 'believers' and 'unbelievers', or between Christianity and other religious traditions, or between the religious and the non-religious, but between those who affirm and contribute to life in the world, and those who do not.

2. Christian mission in the twenty-first century needs to be focused on spirituality, rather than apologetics

We do not live in a godless or totally secularized society. We live in a pluralist society in which most of the world's faiths are represented. Also, many people outside formal religion feel that their life has been touched by the transcendent and seek to respond to this ... The challenge to the Church is to recognize the profile of this kind of burgeoning spirituality ... Christianity should not have to ride roughshod over expressions of contemporary spirituality, for there is a capacity for a dynamic and interactive relationship between the two.[13]

When I say that the emphasis needs to shift from apologetics (rational argumentation to validate belief in God) to spirituality, I am not suggesting that there is no longer a need for an apologetic presentation of the Christian message; this will always be necessary. I am simply saying that there has been a change of context: contrary to expectations, what we are witnessing in so-called 'secular' societies is 'a return of the spiritual impulse.'[14] In a survey for the BBC in 2000, 76 per cent of the British population admitted to having had a spiritual experience – a 59 per cent increase in little more than a decade.[15] My own anecdotal experience suggests that many people are not looking for compelling evidence that God exists; their hunger is much more directed towards spiritual experience and spiritual vitality. There is a vast pool of religion-less spirituality within Western societies, and we cannot expect to see Christianity flourish if we fail to interact positively with this.

As we have already noted, what many people are looking for is a sense of the numinous or the mysterious. 'If religion wants to have a future', David Tacey writes, 'it must allow itself to be seen not only as an institution, but also as a mystery that can feed and nourish the spiritually starving world.' Many people see religion merely as an empty shell, he says; in order to survive, 'it will need to reach into itself, and reveal the mystery that forms the basis of its light and wisdom'. The community will always be receptive to mystery if it can be expressed in valid and contemporary ways.[16]

What does this mean in practice? Tacey argues that churches need to shift from being places of 'devotional worship' to become 'centres of existential spirituality'.[17] By 'devotional worship', Tacey is referring to forms of worship that are controlled and ordered, but spiritless. So what is needed for churches to become centres of existential spirituality? I don't think it means that liturgy must be scrapped. It means that liturgy needs to have more of the feel of being a spiritual practice than a formal ceremony. With words, with silence, with gestures, with actions, with movement, with human contact, with images, with symbols and with sacraments, people need to feel that they are re-entering the sacred mystery of God's loving presence. And to depart feeling cleansed, inspired, stimulated, renewed – re-Spirited.

At St Luke's we have also attempted to become a centre of existential spirituality by creating a programme of events that will not only nourish the spiritual life of regular churchgoers, but also connect with 'the scattered community' of spiritual seekers and pilgrims. 'Breathing Space' includes a regular 'drawing room' where people can explore art as meditation, use workshops on different approaches to prayer, poetry evenings and concerts, Enneagram workshops to deepen self-awareness and nurture personal and spiritual growth, yoga classes, spiritual direction, discussions about the meaning of Christianity for us today, and much more.

A great deal of contemporary spirituality is conditioned by the privatized, consumer-driven culture of postmodernity that inspires people to 'pick and mix' from different sources. Ultimately, this is not sustainable, resulting in spiritual journeys marked by isolation and fragmentation. However, David Tacey believes that beneath the individualized facade of popular spirituality lies a yearning for fellowship and community. It is the innate human need for community, he thinks, that will build religion again. But in order to move towards this, a fresh marriage is required between spirit and religion: 'When religion gets into a new relationship with spirit, it will cease to be experienced as a burden, and begin to be experienced as a personal liberation.'[18] The recovery of Spirited Christianity is essential to the future of Christian mission.

3. Christian mission in the twenty-first century needs to be holistic rather than dualistic

Early in the 1990s I attended a clergy gathering promoting the Decade of Evangelism. After the presentation, when questions were invited, I asked if there would be any good news for the environment in the Decade of Evangelism. In the stunned silence that followed, with forty blank faces gaping at me, I sensed I had just stepped over a line; clearly, 'gospel' and 'trees' should never be mentioned in the same sentence!

Several years before this, when I jointly organized a large gathering of charismatic Christians, I invited Jonathon Porritt, the then Director of Friends of the Earth, to give a keynote address. Jonathon brought an inspiring presentation about the importance of people of faith caring for God's creation, during the course of which he mentioned 'mother earth' (following the example of St Francis of Assisi, of course). At the end of the evening I was swamped with people rebuking me for introducing the New Age into God's house. Nothing I have ever done has elicited such aggressively negative reaction. Nothing I have ever done has left me surer that I made the correct decision.

Hopefully, things have moved on a little since then. Yet I fear that all too often, even where concerns about the environment – or poverty, or social justice – do make it onto the Church's agenda, they are there as add-ons to lend credibility to the gospel rather than as real gospel concerns in and of themselves.

But caring for the earth, making poverty history, combating the AIDS pandemic, supporting fair trade, making peace instead of war, creating social justice, eliminating corruption, and opposing prejudice and bigotry *are* all gospel concerns. Mission is about turning God's liberating love into a flesh-and-blood reality for all creation. 'The Holy Spirit's wave of salvation embraces the whole of life and everything living, and cannot be confined to religion or spirituality.'[19]

By the same token, the gospel of Christ is good news for the whole person: body, mind and spirit. The notion of 'saving souls' as some disembodied entities is a woeful distortion of the *missio dei*. The promise of Pentecost is that God's Spirit, the life-force of the resurrection, is 'poured out on all flesh'. 'This doesn't just mean people's souls. It means their bodies too. It doesn't mean just the "flesh" of human beings: it means the "flesh" of everything living.'[20] The gospel is God's 'Yes' to all life.

The sort of dualistic thinking that has led to the idea of 'saving souls' rather than saving whole persons stems not from the original sources of Christianity but from Gnostic influences in the early centuries of the Church. Gnosticism viewed the material world, including the human body, as inherently evil. And while the early church leaders repudiated this thinking, its influence persisted throughout the centuries. Indeed, much of Christianity has been characterized by spirit/matter dualism. And the effects have been devastating in producing a narrow, guilt-laden pietism that is ill at ease with the body, with sexuality, with femininity, with nature.

Yet Christianity is a religion of incarnation, placing a high value on matter, on flesh, on the physical. In Christ, God took an earthly body, became one with matter, impregnated the material with the divine. Therefore, Christian spirituality should not be understood as a vision of the human soul rising above the material world to encounter the divine in some supra-mundane realm; but rather, as a vision of humanity encountering the divine within the physical and material world. This is the incarnational–sacramental principle, which is so fundamental to Christian understanding.

This holistic nature of Christian spirituality has never been more pertinent or significant than it is within the emerging culture of the twenty-first century:

- In a stressful world, self-esteem and self-worth have become key factors in people's search for spiritual meaning, and this is allied to a need to feel good about one's physical and mental well-being.
- In an age of climate change, the environmental anguish of the earth has penetrated human consciousness, evoking a sense of the profound interconnectedness and interdependence of all life. The needs of the planet and the needs of the person have become one.
- In a media-shrunk global community, the poor world is in the living-room of the rich world. It is impossible to live in isolation.

It essential that Christian mission finds holistic expression by:

- proclaiming God's unconditional love in Jesus Christ;
- feeding the hungry;
- seeking justice for the poor and the disadvantaged;
- taking social responsibility in the community;
- caring for the environment;
- confronting prejudice and discrimination;
- living generously;
- celebrating life.

For you love all things that exist,
and detest none of the things that you have made,
for you would not have made anything if you had hated it.
How would anything have endured if you had not willed
    it?
Or how would anything not called forth by you have been
    preserved?
You spare all things, for they are yours,

O Lord, you who love the living.
For your immortal spirit is in all things.

(The Wisdom of Solomon, 11.24—12.1)

4. Christian mission in the twenty-first century needs to be dialogical rather than monological.

How does one relate to God? How does one relate to other people and to nature? These are the questions that Martin Buber, the great Jewish philosopher, sought to answer in his seminal book, *I and Thou*.[21] Fundamentally, Buber argues that through authentic relationships with men and women, we can come to know the eternal 'Thou' – God.

His essay sets out a typology to identify two distinct modes of relating. In the I–It mode we treat the other person as an object or an 'it' upon whom to impose our own will and purpose. There is no real relationship. The other person is boxed and categorized in our mind – a 'black', a 'gay', a 'homophobe', a 'liberal', a 'fundamentalist', a 'woman', and so on. We then see, hear and judge that person through the lens of our own prejudiced perspectives. In contrast to the I–It mode of interacting, Buber identifies an I–Thou form of relationship in which we recognize and treat the other person as a whole being, a free person who is not labelled or categorized, but seen and heard in his or her own right. Such an encounter, Buber believed, is never simply between two persons: every 'thou' encounter provides glimpses through to the eternal 'Thou'.

Buber's model pinpoints what crucially needs to lie at the heart of all Christian mission: an encounter with the divine Thou, mediated through a human I–Thou interaction. Whether mission consists in sharing the good news of Christ verbally, or meeting the needs of the poor, or serving through some social initiative, or campaigning for justice, or mediating in a conflict situation, or planting a church, or caring for the environment, an I–Thou encounter must create the context for all that is said or done.

Yet this is far from being always the case. A massive amount of Christian mission consists in an I–It mode of relating, in which people become objects of evangelism, or of some social initiative, or of some other missionary scheme. This was brought home to me when Jim, the 'unconverted' husband of a woman in a church I led, told me of his past experiences with churches his wife Ruth had attended. He said that whenever he stepped into a church, he felt a syrupy flow of attention directed towards him. 'I was the unconverted husband,' he said, 'so they saw me as a challenge.' But he said that, even as he felt their glow of attention, he also felt strangely rejected. 'I knew they weren't really interested in me as a person,' he said, 'only as a potential convert.' I suspect that Jim is simply articulating what countless thousands of others have felt. I–It expressions of Christian mission are dehumanizing, and ultimately unproductive.

In practice, the I–Thou mode of interacting is created and sustained through dialogue and genuine conversation. But a basic requirement of real dialogue is that both parties are open to receive, to learn, to be enriched by the encounter. In my experience, this is rare in the context of Christian mission – especially evangelism, where the assumption, generally, is that 'I have something to say to you, and you need to listen.' Ann Morisy expresses the point perfectly in her book, *Beyond the Good Samaritan*:

> Unfortunately, dialogue is not a process which is a priority in our churches, and in particular it is often absent in relation to our evangelistic efforts. The assumption at the heart of evangelism is that people will be changed by what Christians tell them or represent to them; it scarcely ever includes the expectation, essential to the process of dialogue, that such a transformation or change in outlook will work both ways ... commitment to dialogue means that Christians involved in community ministry need to be open to the possibility that their faith and their view of the world will be changed as a result of that dialogue.[22]

The essence of dialogue, Ann Morisy says, is that each person who is party to the communication is open to the possibility of being changed by the testimony of the other, in the way that Jesus was prepared to be changed by the words and passionate commitment of the Syro-Phoenician woman. It was at this point that Jesus acknowledges that his mission is as much to the Gentiles as it is to the Jews.[23]

David Tacey throws out the challenge that if the Church wishes to play a role in the future, 'It will have to start listening to the world and discerning the presence of God in it ... The churches should regard dialogue with popular spirituality as part of their ministry and mission.'[24]

It is time to recognize that Christians do not have a monopoly on divine revelation; that God is already in the world in the lives of men and women who may not turn up to church on a Sunday morning, but who can show regular churchgoers a thing or two where God and spiritual reality are concerned. These are the 'scattered community' of believers, doubters, questioners and spiritual pilgrims whom we need to welcome into a Spirited conversation, with the expectation that our faith and our view of the world will be changed, as well as theirs.

I believe that Martin Buber's I–Thou model of human interaction must characterize all Christian mission in the twenty-first century.

5. Christian mission in the twenty-first century needs to find expression through open, empowering church communities

Maureen's daughter died of a drug overdose. When I visited her to discuss the funeral arrangements, she greeted me with an urgent: 'I want the funeral in the church, Dave. I've got to bring her home to *my* church.' Her request – to which I gladly acquiesced – contained the seemingly odd feature that she did not actually attend the church. Indeed, so far as I know, she had never attended a service at St Luke's. Yet she considered it to be her church.

Maureen's story highlights the peculiarity of the Church of England, and its quaint, apparently outdated parish system, whereby, as the vicar of St Luke's, I have the 'cure' of 12,000 people in our little patch of north London. To many people the situation is entirely anachronistic and somewhat absurd, a remnant of a bygone era. Yet, I believe the parish model of church represents a powerful symbol of a kingdom-orientated rather than a church-orientated approach to Christian mission. And it gives a vicar like me untold opportunities to bring God's loving care to people like Maureen. And sometimes such people really do end up making the Church their home.

By describing the parish model of church ministry as a symbol of kingdom-orientated mission, I'm not simply talking about a literal geographical parish, but about a mentality that recognizes and practises an 'open' rather than a 'closed' border approach to Church.

A *closed border* model of Church tends to see Christian commitment arising from a definite conversion experience linked to a decision to 'accept Christ as one's Saviour' and to believe certain doctrines or propositions concerning Christ and the gospel. And the boundary lines are drawn quite clearly around such a community: one is either 'in' or 'out', converted or unconverted, a believer or an unbeliever, redeemed or unredeemed, a Christian or a non-Christian. There may be unconverted people on the fringes, but it is clear that they are not really accepted as insiders to the Church. This model of Church could be characterized by the phrase 'believing before belonging'.

An *open border* model, on the other hand, sees conversion as a process, which may or may not incorporate specific 'experiences' of faith commitment. It is a more journey-orientated vision of Christianity that sits comfortably with shades of grey where faith is concerned. So there is no need to determine who is in or out; conversion is a way of life linked just as much to one's pattern of changing attitudes and to one's life choices as to what one believes – which isn't to say that what one does or does not believe is unimportant: quite the contrary. But it is more important that we learn to trust God, and to live lives shaped by the values and attitudes of God's kingdom than to believe the 'right' things. This model of Church could be characterized by the phrase 'belonging before/without believing'. It is Church that is 'open at the edges', but 'committed at the core', as my friend Mike Riddell puts it.[25]

The 'open border' approach to Church not only offers a genuine welcome to the uninitiated, it also creates a much more liberating environment for those who do consider themselves 'insiders' because it acknowledges that a church community will potentially contain a mixture of people with a wide variety of beliefs and doctrinal positions, and a variety of levels of faith commitment. Even within 'closed border' churches these varieties often exist, but are masked by the constraint to conform to a certain formula of experience and belief.

In my view, an 'open border' policy will also extend to an 'open table' approach to receiving Communion, based on Jesus' practice of generous table fellowship, in which he ate and drank with prostitutes, tax collectors, publicans and general outcasts from a respectable religious society. It is suggested that it was this practice above all else that led to Jesus' crucifixion – he was executed for eating with the wrong people,[26] especially since he did so in the name of the kingdom of God. Practitioners of an 'open table' policy speak of it as 'an imitation of Jesus' risky prophetic hospitality which included and converted those who ate with him'.[27]

Sara Miles bears testimony to the converting power of an open table in her wonderfully inspiring book, *Take This Bread: A Radical Conversion*. Her conversion, she says, began with an outstretched hand to receive Communion. Sara describes herself as a blue-state, secular intellectual, a lesbian, and a left-wing journalist, who had absolutely no intention of becoming a Christian until one day when, with nothing more than a journalist's curiosity, she walked in on a Communion service at St Gregory's Episcopal Church in San Francisco. Someone put a piece of fresh, crumbly bread in her hands, saying 'The body of Christ', and handed her a goblet of sweet wine saying

'The blood of Christ', 'then something outrageous and terrifying happened. Jesus happened to me.' She reflects:

> I still can't explain my first communion. It made no sense. I was in tears and physically unbalanced: I felt as if I had just stepped off a curb, or been knocked over, painlessly, from behind. The disconnect between what I thought was happening – I was eating a piece of bread; what I heard someone else say was happening – the piece of bread was the 'body' of 'Christ', a patently untrue, or at best metaphorical statement; and what I knew was happening – God, named 'Christ' or 'Jesus', was real, and in my mouth – utterly short-circuited my ability to do anything but cry.[28]

From this experience a wonderful adventure opened up for Sara Miles. Inspired by the inclusiveness of Jesus, she wanted to extend the 'open table' policy at St Gregory's to include the poor, undernourished communities around the church. So she set up a food pantry offering groceries (not meals) to hundreds of families each week. But she is very clear: this is not a social programme, it is an extension of Communion. So the food is served from the eucharistic altar and from tables around the altar. It is Communion in a bag of groceries – 'the body of Christ!'

But it is even more than this: St Gregory's food pantry is a 'companionship of empowerment', where the recipients of the food then become the organizers of the project. It is a kind of 'political practice' that not only feeds but also empowers.

> We had homeless guys and women with missing teeth and a couple who spoke Tagalog come join us; a transsexual with a thick Bronx accent, some teenagers, an ancient Greek woman from across the street, and a dapper man from St Gregory's choir who came and played the accordion during the pantry. They were all people who, like me, had come to get fed and stayed to help out. Who, like me, took that bread and got changed. We were all converting: turning into new people as we rubbed up against one another.[29]

In a fractured and fragmented world where many starve for relationships, the capacity to offer a place in which to belong is an immense asset for the Church. I have already quoted David Tacey making the comment that, 'It is this innate human need for community that will build religion again.' But it needs to be 'kingdom-styled' community, which is inclusive and affirming, liberating and empowering; where people can belong and contribute to the overall life of the community without necessarily feeling able to tick certain doctrinal boxes. Once we treat conversion as a process, and allow identity to be governed by participation rather than doctrine, some very liberating and attractive forms of Church can begin to emerge: 'Church is then an open community of people who are endeavoring to help each other along the Way.'[30]

Christian mission in the twenty-first century requires kingdom-orientated communities, places of radical inclusion and empowerment, which say: You are welcome – whatever your ethnic or cultural background, however you look or dress, whether you are a man or a woman, gay or straight, whether you earn a pittance or you're worth a fortune, whether you have kids, can't have kids, don't want to have kids, whether you are full of faith or riddled with doubts, whether you feel hopeful or fearful. Gregarious or withdrawn – YOU ARE WELCOME!

Notes

1 Stephen R. Covey, *The Seven Habits of Highly Effective People*, London: Simon & Schuster, 1992, pp. 106, 136–9.

2 David Tacey, *The Spirituality Revolution: The Emergence of Contemporary Spirituality*, Hove: Brunner-Routledge, 2004, p. 36f.

3 Jürgen Moltmann, *The Source of Life: The Holy Spirit and the Theology of Life*, London: SCM Press, 1997, p. 19.

4 Moltmann, *The Source*, p. 20.

5 John Dominic Crossan, 'Jesus and the Kingdom', in Marcus Borg (ed.), *Jesus at 2000*, Oxford: Westview Press, 1997, p. 33f.

6 Marcus Borg, *The Heart of Christianity: How We Can Be Passionate Believers Today*, New York: HarperCollins, 2003, p. 132.

7 Crossan, 'Jesus', p. 33.

8 Crossan, 'Jesus', p. 42.

9 Crossan, 'Jesus', p. 42.

10 This phrase was used by Pope John Paul II and is quoted in Moltmann, *The Source*, p. 20.

11 David J. Bosch, *Transforming Mission: Paradigm Shifts in Theology of Mission*, New York: Orbis Books, 1995, p. 390.

12 John Henson, *Good as New: A Radical Retelling of the Scriptures*, New York: Basic Books, 2004, p. 392.

13 Mission Theological Group, *The Search For Faith and the Witness of the Church*, London: Church House Publishing, 1996, p. 74f.

14 David Tacey, *The Spirituality*, p. 12.

15 David Hay and Kate Hunt, 'Is Britain Waking Up?', in *The Tablet*, London, 24 June, 2000, p. 846 .

16 David Tacey, *The Spirituality Revolution*, p. 190f.

17 David Tacey, *The Spirituality Revolution*, p. 193.

18 David Tacey, *The Spirituality Revolution*, p. 19ff.

19 Moltmann, *The Source*, p. 22.

20 Moltmann, *The Source*, p. 71.

21 Martin Buber, *I And Thou*, Edinburgh: T. & T. Clark, 1937.

22 Ann Morisy, *Beyond the Good Samaritan: Community Ministry and Mission*, London: Mowbray, 1997, p. 63.

23 Morisy, *Beyond*, p. 65.

24 Tacey, *The Spirituality Revolution*, p. 195.

25 Michael Riddell, *Threshold of the Future: Reforming the Church in the Post-Christian West*, London: SPCK, 1998, p. 150.

26 Norman Perrin, *Rediscovering the Teaching of Jesus*, London: SCM Press, 1967, p. 102ff.

27 Donald Schell, 'Breaking Barriers: Rethinking our Theology of Baptism', in *Open: Journal of the Associated Parishes for Liturgy and Mission*, Vol. 48, No. 2, p. 7.

28 Sara Miles, *Take This Bread: A Radical Conversion – The Spiritual Memoir of a Twenty-First Century Christian*, New York: Ballentine Press, 2007, p. 58f.

29 Miles, *Take This Bread*, p. 138.

30 Riddell, *Threshold*, p. 150.